Architecture In Virginia

An Official Guide to
Four Centuries of Building in the Old Dominion

by William B. O'Neal,
Chairman,
Division of Architectural History,
University of Virginia

Published for the
Virginia Museum
by Walker & Company, Inc.
New York

First Edition

D1267985

The Virginia Museum, our nation's first Statewide arts agency, is hereby authorized to prepare and publish a guide to the most significant examples of the architecture of this Commonwealth, from Jamestown to Reston. The book, in both paperback and hardcover editions, will be entitled *Architecture in Virginia: An Official Guide to Four Centuries of Building in the Old Dominion.*

The illustrated guide, assembled with the aid and advice of recognized authorities, should be a valuable reference for teachers and students, a helpful companion to travelers from within and without the State, and a source of pleasure and pride for all Virginians.

Mills E. Godwin, Jr., *Governor*
The Commonwealth of Virginia

The Virginia Museum's unique legislative mandate, "to promote throughout the Commonwealth education in the realm of art," has long been interpreted to include all the arts.

For more than thirty years, the Museum has been singularly successful in circulating throughout the State not only the static arts of painting, sculpture and decoration (via its State Services Program and its now widely imitated Artmobiles), but also the performing arts of drama, music and dance (via its Statewide Theatre Arts System).

The Museum properly honors significant contemporary Virginia buildings via biennial exhibitions chosen by juries of nationally known authorities. But architecture has always been difficult to present in a gallery setting. Buildings must be directly experienced to be fully appreciated.

Therefore, with the creation of this first guide to Virginia's rare heritage, the Museum fills a long-standing need, for architecture, the long-recognized "Mother of the Arts," is the Old Dominion's pre-eminent indigenous artistic expression.

It is a special pleasure, then, to the Trustees and Staff of the Museum (greatly aided by the Advisory Board) to comply with the Governor's request to produce this volume, which we believe to be the first such guide issued by a Statewide arts agency.

Leslie Cheek, Jr.

Leslie Cheek, Jr., *Director*
The Virginia Museum

Table of Contents

How To Use This Book

This volume is a guide to Virginia architecture, not a history of it. It does not pretend to be exhaustive or complete. Rather, an attempt has been made to choose fine examples of each type of structure that has played an important part in the development of building in the State.

The chief criterion for inclusion is architectural excellence, not historical association. To be chosen, moreover, a building must have architectural significance beyond its immediate locale, either on the State or the national level. Finally, with two exceptions too important to omit (Rosewell and Barboursville), eligible buildings must have been in existence at press time.

The book is divided into six sections corresponding to six convenient geographical areas of the State. Within these sections, buildings are grouped by counties and towns in alphabetical order. Within each county and town, sites are listed alphabetically by name.

Simplified maps are provided at the front and back of the book and at the beginning of each section. For more detailed information, the reader should obtain a standard highway map.

As admission charges change from time to time, exact prices have not been indicated. Most sites, however, charge only a modest fee. Similarly, open hours may vary, and the traveler is advised to confirm these times before setting out. Sites not open to the public are designated "private."

Despite the time and care expended on the preparation of this book, some errors are inevitable in a project of such scope. The publishers will be grateful for having these called to their attention, so that corrections may be made in future editions.

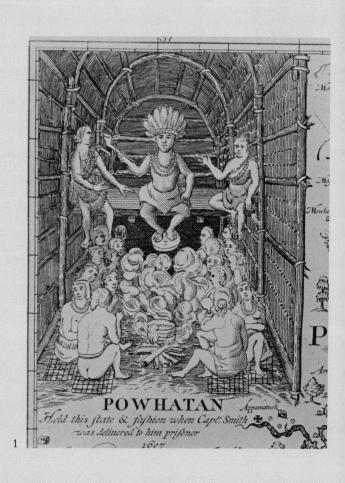

Introduction

When the first colonists reached Virginia they found that the Indians sometimes used light wicker-work structures, a sort of primitive version of the colonists' own late medieval wattle and daub (woven branches covered with mud as in the reconstructions at the Jamestown Festival Park). But the newcomers were far more interested in the land itself than in such bits of exotic architecture as they might find.

John Smith described this land as a "country that may have the prerogative over the most pleasant places of Europe, Asia, Africa, or America, for large and pleasant navigable rivers: heaven and earth never agreed better to frame a place for man's habitation being of our constitutions, were it fully manured and inhabited by industrious people. Here are mountains, hills, plains, valleys, rivers and brooks all running most pleasantly into a fair bay compassed, but for the mouth, with fruitful and delightsome land."

During his first visit with the Indians, Smith discovered that tobacco was one of the products of this "delightsome land." He records that "there was joy in my heart to find here green gold, so much in demand by the merchants of London that its value is as great as the most precious metals." Within a very short time of the first landing, then, the principal characteristics and resources of the colony were discovered and defined —the rivers, the rich land and the tobacco.

Architecture, in the European sense, also played a most important part in the early days of the colony. Powhatan, the Indian sachem, was apparently envious of the Jamestown buildings, ill-constructed as they were, for, when the settlement was in need of food in December of 1608, he offered to barter one hundred and fifty hogsheads of corn in return for a house similar to Ratcliffe's "palace," the largest building there. Smith, himself, worked on this structure for Powhatan for twelve hours a day until it had to be abandoned due to a plot against the Captain's life.

Not much remains to us from the 17th century, and it is

1   *John Smith's map of Virginia shows an Indian structure c. 1607.*

2   *Latrobe's 1798 sketch of Green Spring, c. 1645, at Jamestown.*

2

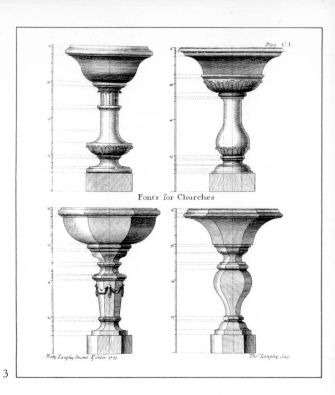

Fonts for Churches

Batty Langley Invent & delin 1739

Tho' Langley Sculp

3

4

8   Architecture in Virginia

almost impossible to gain any general knowledge of the state of architecture during this time in the colony. We do know that the last quarter of the century saw enough prosperity to allow a certain expansiveness to enter into those buildings that served for more than mere shelter. We know, from a very few extant examples, that the shaped gable was still being used long after it had been abandoned in England, and we also know that the builders of the colony were beginning to come to terms with the un-English climate found here by placing their chimneys on the outside walls and frequently keeping their houses only one room deep in order to take advantage of every breeze.

The rusticity of mid-17th century building is well illustrated by Sir William Berkeley's "wilderness palace" begun c. 1645. Upset at Jamestown's primitive lack of facilities, he began a huge country house which was called by his widow in 1678 "the finest seat in America and the only tollerable place for a Governor." Now demolished, Green Spring, as the house was called, may be studied in Benjamin Henry Latrobe's sketch of 1798, which shows a large but dilapidated and very "country" kind of building with a Jacobean gable as the central feature of the front porch.

But the really important architectural event of this period was the removal of the capital from Jamestown to Williamsburg at the very end of the 17th century. Though superseding a small settlement, Williamsburg was, in effect, a new town, and was planned without the constrictions of an island site or the needs of defense, as was Jamestown.

The ambition and vision of Williamburg's planners are symbolized by the large and elaborate building for the College of William and Mary, the first of many elaborate and lavish public buildings to be erected there.

Though still provincial in the sense of being about a genera-

5

3 Copein, mason for Pohick Church, was asked to carve a font from a design on this plate, No. 150 in Langley's "The City and County Builder's and Workman's Treasury of Designs," London, 1740.

4 Early editions of Salmon's "Palladio Londinensis; or, the London Art of Building" greatly influenced many Virginia interiors. Such paneling as that at Tazewell Hall shows the influence of plates like this, No. 13 from the 7th edition, London, 1767.

5 Langley's Plate 170 is a possible prototype for the decorated plaster ceilings of mid-18th century Virginia, as at Kenmore.

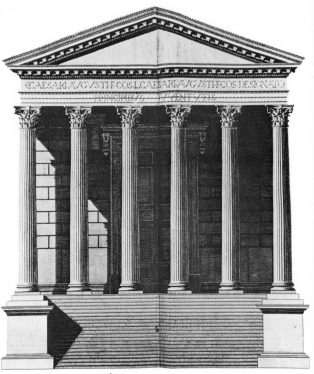

Façade de la maison quarrée à Nismes

6

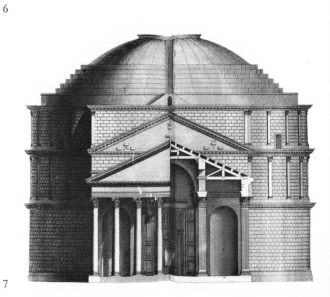

7

tion behind the mother country in the usage of architectural forms, the colony, in establishing a *new* metropolitan center, took the first step to close that provincial gap, which by the time of the Revolution had ceased to exist for all practical purposes.

The speed of this development may be judged from contemporary accounts. Hugh Jones wrote that Williamsburg, c. 1722, was built with "brick, but most commonly with timber lined with cieling, and cased with feather-edged plank, painted with white lead and oil, covered with shingles of cedar, etc. tarred over at first; with a passage generally through the middle of the house for an air-draught in summer," a description that makes Williamsburg seem still a village.

But in 1765, only forty-three years later, a French traveler described the life of the planters in a way that sounds very sophisticated indeed. He wrote, "there are many of them who have very great Estates, but are mostly at loss for Cash. They live very well haveing all the necessaries on their Estates in great plenty. Madeira wine and punch made with Jamaica rum is their Chief Drink. There are no large towns in this province, by reason of the Conveniency of its many navaiguable rivers, by which ships go up to all parts of it to the planters Doors: the Chief of thos reside Mostley on the Borders of James and York rivers which is the best soil for tobacco Especially the Sweet sented which is so much Esteemed in England, where they keep it for their own use, or what they Call home Consumption. the other sort Called aranoacke, is Exported to Holland, Denmark, Sweden, and Germany."

The rivers, the land and the tobacco still dominated the life of the colony, though the plantation houses were changing to reflect the new sophistication. From the sturdy, solid mass of the early Georgian ones of the first part of the 18th century, they were becoming more Palladian, more graceful and more finely detailed during the century's third quarter.

By this time the plans had changed from the central mass of the main house with detached dependencies to the more architectonic one of the central mass of the house with its dependencies attached, the attaching wings often assuming a curved plan as at Mount Airy. Also by this time more recent information was being imported in the form of books, which gave the colonist a documentary source of architectural knowledge rather than a purely remembered one, as in the 17th century.

The coming of the Revolution not only slowed down building operations, but also forced the removal of the capital of the

6   *The Maison Carré at Nimes was Jefferson's inspiration for the Capitol at Richmond. This plate, No. 2, is from "Antiquités de la France," Paris, 1778, a book of measured drawings issued by Jefferson's collaborator on the Capitol, Charles-Louis Clérisseau.*

7   *This drawing of the Pantheon, Plates 56 and 57, Book 4, of "The Architecture of A. Palladio in Four Books . . . Revis'd, Design'd, and Publish'd by Giacomo Leoni," London, 1721, was used by Thomas Jefferson in designing the Rotunda of the University of Virginia.*

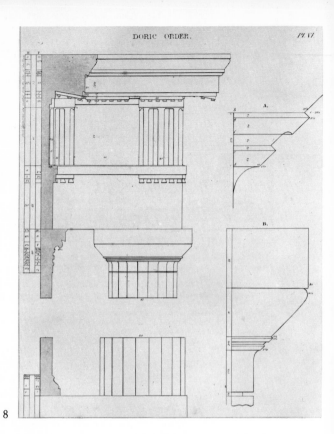

8

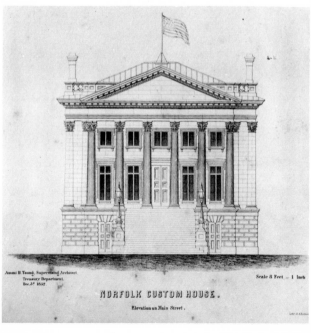

NORFOLK CUSTOM HOUSE.

Elevation on Main Street.

Ammi B. Young, Supervising Architect.
Treasury Department.
Dec. 3ʳᵈ 1857.

Scale 8 Feet = 1 Inch

9

12 Architecture in Virginia

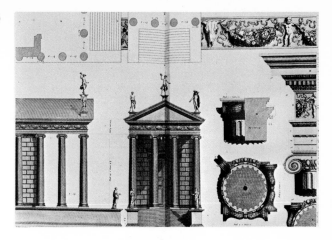

8   This plate, No. 6 in Asher Benjamin's "The Builder's Guide, or Complete System of Architecture," Boston, 1843, is a possible source for the orders of Greek Revival houses like Linden Row.

9   Ammi B. Young's drawing of the Norfolk Customs House, lithographed by August Kollner, a German who worked in Philadelphia.

10   The source of the order for Pavilion II of the University of Virginia is found in Plates 35, 36 and 37 of Leoni's "Palladio."

new Commonwealth from Williamsburg to Richmond. Williamsburg, falling into poverty, was happily preserved for us by this move, as only prosperous cities tear down old buildings to make way for the new.

The Revolution saw, as well, the disestablishment of the church. As a result many of the small country parish churches were abandoned and fell into grave disrepair. Worse still, this beautiful architectural type, which was so peculiarly a development of the colonial period, ceased to be built for a great many years indeed.

After the Revolution, a columnar neo-classicism was introduced into Virginia with Jefferson's Capitol. The Georgian strain in architecture began to disappear in the refinements and simplicities of the Federal Period, a style contemporary with neo-classicism.

The 19th century, begun on this surge of confident neo-classicism, saw Virginia well in the forefront of those movements that ruled the world of architecture during the 1800's. It was a century of revivals—Egyptian, Greek, Roman, Gothic, the Italianate, the picturesque, Romanesque and even Romanesque-Byzantine—and all were to be found in Virginia, as well as throughout the western world. But it was also a century of discovery and expansion, both necessary for the support of the increasing population and its demands for shelter for its various activities.

The 19th century was rent asunder by the Civil War, but the renewed activity in building after the war was both vigorous and visionary. It is best illustrated, perhaps, by the iron-

11

12

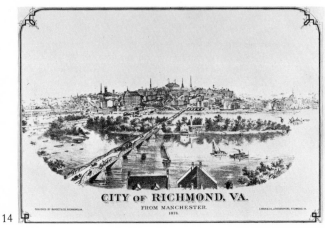

13

CITY OF RICHMOND, VA.
FROM MANCHESTER.
1876.

14

14 Architecture in Virginia

fronted business blocks put up in Richmond in 1866, only a few months after the disastrous Evacuation Fire.

The 19th was also the century of the emergence of the architect as a known and noted personage. From the time of Jefferson and Latrobe at the beginning of the century until the employment of Stanford White to restore Jefferson's Rotunda at the University of Virginia after its fire in 1895, Virginians did not hesitate to engage the best architects they could find.

But the 19th century ended as the century in which the traditional rural organization of the Commonwealth had been destroyed. The use of the rivers as highways began to decline, while the new railroads provided swift and easy land transportation and served the increasingly important cities. The land and tobacco were still the basis of the State's wealth, but industrialization began to set the stage for the 20th century.

The new century began on a high tide of eclecticism, tempered by an informed clientele and an able body of architects. This movement reached its climax in the series of beautiful neo-Georgian houses built in many areas of the state by William Lawrence Bottomley between the two World Wars.

During these years, however, modern methods and modern forms were introduced, usually commissioned, interestingly enough, by far-seeing industrialists. After the second war, this trend became vigorous and vital due to new materials, a new prosperity and the demands for new building types.

Tradition is strong in Virginia, but it is also resilient and adaptable. Virginians, for example, have always demanded noble buildings for their educational institutions, a tradition unbroken from the College of William and Mary to the new

11   *In 1817 the Capitol dominated Richmond as from an acropolis.*

12   *A Currier & Ives lithograph entitled "The Fall of Richmond, Va., on the Night of April 2d., 1865" suggests the vast ruin.*

13   *A. W. Warren made this sketch, "East Main St., April 2-3, 1865," for "Harper's Weekly," which published it on April 22.*

14   *A lithograph by A. Hoen & Co., dated 1867, indicates the vigor with which Richmond rebuilt its central area after the war.*

15   *The Jefferson's Grand Salon was pale green, ivory and gold.*

15

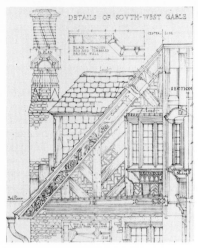

16

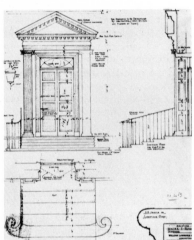

17

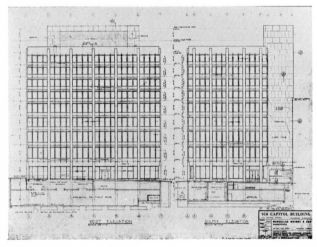

18

16 Architecture in Virginia

public schools of 1966 in Charlottesville.

Hospitality in the Old Dominion has resulted in a long series of splendid residences of infinite variety from the early plantation houses to the recently built house by Richard Neutra in Richmond. This tradition of hospitality also resulted in a group of inns, springs, hotels and motels that catered to the visual pleasure of their guests as well as to their comfort.

Traditionally in Virginia, buildings housing civil governments have been developed beyond the utilitarian. This tradition, of course, has given us not only a remarkable group of 18th and 19th century courthouses, but, just yesterday, the very beautiful City Hall complex in Norfolk by Vincent Kling.

The tradition of Virginia's rivers has renewed itself, for they are now serving as highways for industry. Her land, never rejected, now supports one of her largest commercial endeavors in her timbering industry. And tobacco, never having lost its importance, is still a source of "green gold," both in manufacturing and agriculture.

But perhaps one of the most interesting traditions to have survived is that given the first settlers by the London Company. They were told that as "order is the same price with confusion" they should plan ordered towns. This instruction has been carried out, in large part, throughout the four centuries of Virginia's growth. The latest example of the implementation of this precept is the New Town of Reston, where order, vision, planning and intelligence have given a new dimension to the Commonwealth's oldest architectural tradition.

16 *Pope's drawing of the southwest gable of the Branch House.*

17 *William Lawrence Bottomley's drawing for a doorway of Milburne, the Walter S. Robertson house, 315 Locke Lane, Richmond.*

18 *Elevations of the Life of Virginia Building in it first phase. Later additions and alterations will fill its entire city block.*

19 *A preliminary drawing by Wright of the Pope-Leighey House.*

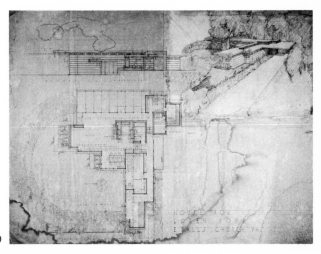

19

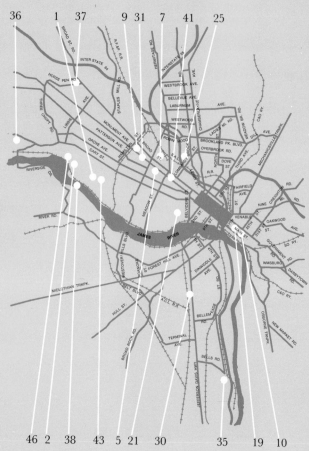

Section A   The Richmond Area   Introduction

Richmond, established by William Byrd II, remained a small town until the capital of the Commonwealth was moved there in 1780. From that time on, it spread and grew, supported by the needs of government and industry. It is especially rich in monuments of the 19th century, all of whose architectural revivals are well illustrated in the city. In fact, it would be possible to gain some insight into the entire history of architecture through a study of these revival buildings, beginning with the Egyptian Building at the Medical College of Virginia. But one must hurry, for, like all prosperous cities, Richmond has demolished many of her early buildings, over 1500 pre-1850 ones, it is estimated, since 1945!

Richmond is also a city of cast iron of such excellence that it easily surpasses cities rather better known for this feature. The working of iron was a very early industry in Virginia, having been established at Falling Water in 1619 on the Ampthill plantation. Richmond's cast iron industry reached its peak in the 19th century, but the tradition of metal working is now continued in the 20th century aluminum industry.

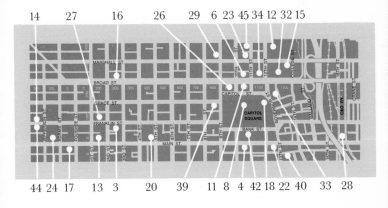

A1

A2

A3

A4

A1   **Agecroft Hall** *late 15th century; 1926   4395 Sulgrave Rd.   Private*

Mr. and Mrs. Thomas C. Williams, Jr., in 1926, brought Agecroft Hall to Richmond and had it rebuilt on its present site. It
had originally overlooked the Irwell River just outside Manchester in England and was a particularly good example of the
late 15th century half-timbered manor house. Its reincarnation
in Richmond is indeed a very happy one, for its crisp black and
white patterns and its picturesque massing are especially well
settled in its new location. The house is now owned by the
Richmond Foundation.

A2   **Ampthill** *1732; 1750; 1929; 1951   211 Ampthill Rd.   Private*

Ampthill, built by and for (and presumably designed by)
Henry Cary, II, was located in Chesterfield Co. Cary, under
whose supervision many Williamsburg public buildings were
erected, began his house with a simple center-hall, single-room-
on-either-side plan. Later rooms were added behind each existing room, making a U-shaped plan with a narrow central court.
This central court was filled in, and detached dependencies
were added, about 1750, after the death of Henry Cary, II. The
house was moved to Richmond in 1929, at which time the dependencies, originally a kitchen and a ballroom, were attached
to the main house. In 1951 the present dormers were added to
the hip-on-hip roof. The paneling of Ampthill is especially fine,
with the dining room being the best of the first-floor rooms. It
is now owned by Mr. and Mrs. D. Tennant Bryan.

A3   **Bolling Haxall House** *1858; 1884; c. 1900   211 E. Franklin St.*
Private

The 1850's in Richmond saw the transition from the romantic
classicism of the Greek Revival to the full gusto of Victorianism,
of which this house is a splendid example. Its use of iron in the
lintels, the porch railings and the beautiful fence, probably by
George Lownes, its elongated cupola, its extraordinary semi-
circular "pediment" over the central third story window, its
paneled facade, and its heavy, bracketed entablature are all
characteristic features of the new movement. A later owner replaced the stairway in 1884 by one of solid walnut "which is
said to have cost over $3,000 . . ," and "the walls on the main
floor are handsomely frescoed," according to a contemporary
newspaper report. In 1900 the house was sold to the Woman's
Club of Richmond, which added the auditorium at the rear
shortly thereafter.

A4   **Branch & Co.** *1866   1015 E. Main St.   Private*

After the great Richmond fire at the end of the Civil War, there
was a vast need for new business buildings. It is notable that the
Virginia Fire and Marine Insurance Co. was able to put up
this handsome, iron-fronted structure as early as 1866. Not only
have its iron elements been combined into a façade of singular
interest, but its unknown architect anticipated the split-level

A5

A6

A7

A8

use of floors in a remarkably successful way. The building is now owned by Branch & Co.

A5   **Branch House** *1916   2501 Monument Ave.   By appointment*

John Kerr Branch, who began his collection of the decorative arts at nineteen with two 16th century chairs, started this largest and most elaborate of Richmond's town houses in 1916 as a setting for that collection. He chose as his architect John Russell Pope, of whom it was said that he could "give renewed value to an old and perfectly formed style." In the Branch house he certainly gave "renewed value" to the Tudor style, inventing, within its limits, all the spaces necessary to care for life on so expansive a scale. These refinements of service called for a large number of storage rooms, each for a special purpose, such as trunks or rugs, and even a second boiler to be used if the operating one failed. Although the house nominally has three stories, it has eleven levels, which, surprisingly, are all supported on fireproof concrete. No detail was neglected nor was any detail poorly executed. The house, now the property of the United Givers' Fund of Richmond, has easily adapted its large and small spaces to its new uses.

A6   **Broad Street Methodist Church** *1860   Broad & 10th Sts.*

A strong movement is underway to save this abandoned and badly defaced building. Designed by Albert L. West, it originally had a very tall and exaggeratedly thin spire crowning its entrance porch. When this became dangerous it was removed, removing at the same time the excitement and dominance of the church in the urban scene. The building, as it stands, is still full of interest for its Victorian vigor in both plan and the adaptation of classic detail.

A7   **Broad Street Station** *1919   Broad & Robinson Sts.*

When John Russell Pope designed the Broad Street Station in 1919, he gave back to the city the serenity of classic forms put to commercial uses. Although it may be an anomaly to set the dome of the Pantheon on top of tracks used by Diesel engines, it was a practice in the best eclectic tradition. In any case, one's spirit is soothed the moment one walks into the nobly proportioned waiting room. Is this not most useful, one might almost say functional, in the hurry of a train arrival or departure?

The building gains in effectiveness from its careful use of natural materials, the ease with which large crowds may be handled within it, and the wisdom of the owners and architect in selecting a site that afforded adequate parking space—now the constant and constantly unsolved problem of urban living. It is owned by the Richmond Terminal Railway Company.

A8   **Capitol Square** *1785; 1819; 1824   Capitol open Mon.-Fri. 8:15-5, Sat. 9-5, Sun. 1:30-5:30*

In old prints Capitol Square in Richmond appears as a kind of acropolis, rising above the James River with great dignity to

A8

A9

A10

24 Architecture in Virginia

the climax of its temple-form Capitol, which, designed in 1785 by Thomas Jefferson in collaboration with the Frenchman Charles-Louis Clérisseau, introduced neo-classicism into public building in America. At about the same time Jean-Antoine Houdon journeyed to this country to undertake the portrait of Washington that still stands in the Capitol here. Thus, Capitol Square began its existence with two masterpieces.

The Capitol, which was originally built without steps leading up to its portico, has been much changed over the years. Not only have the extensions for the two houses of the legislature been added, but the plan of the central building now lacks one of the original legislative chambers. The many extensions and remodelings have hidden most of the original fabric, but, fortunately, Jefferson's and Clérisseau's intentions may be clearly seen in the model sent from France as a guide for the erection of the building.

The next important addition to Capitol Square was the magnificent cast iron fence enclosing it. Although its designer, Paul-Alexis Sabbaton, had worked in Richmond, he had removed to New York by the time he won the competition for the fence, which, with its spears and fasces, was cast there, shipped to Richmond by water, and set up on its granite base in 1819.

The bell tower replaced an earlier, wooden one in 1824. It was built for the Virginia Public Guard and was used as a guardhouse for some time, as well as a signal tower for emergencies and meetings. Its rather bland Federalist design, amazingly enough, seems to have given some aesthetic offence during the 1870's, but it has happily survived and is now being restored as a museum and headquarters for the First Virginia Regiment.

A9　**Central National Bank** *1957　3501 W. Broad St.　Banking hours*

This award-winning building, commissioned in February, 1956, from Baskervill and Son, Hankins and Anderson, brought many innovations to the area. Its exposed steel, grey brick, and blue and gold anodized aluminum mark an early use of those materials in such a combination in Richmond. The booths for the drive-in tellers are connected with the building by tunnels. But most interesting is the fact that its vertical louvres, probably the first to have been installed in Richmond, are controlled by clock work geared to sun time.

A10　**Church Hill Restoration** *c. 1800-1850; 1958　near St. John's Church, Broad and 27th Sts.*

A remarkable restoration and preservation project is being carried out in Richmond. An area filled with original houses and centering on St. John's Church was declared an Historic Zone in 1958, and the Historic Richmond Foundation has supervised the rehabilitation and restoration carried out here. The extraordinary aspect of the work is that no public money has been used (except on public works: a fire station and a park). The Foundation, its friends and private owners finance the work. Several square blocks have been brought back to

A11

A12

life in this way, and the area, high on its bluff above the James, has become an exemplar of 19th century architecture in Richmond.

Even St. John's, as it now stands, is largely 19th century. Finished first in 1741, the present east-west transepts represent the original building, and, if any colonial work remains, it is in the weatherboarding of the walls of the transepts and the brick of their foundations. Much work seems to have been done between 1830 and 1903, when the present tower, the last of three, was erected.

Of the houses in the area the following are notable, but by no means does this list exhaust the points of interest: Turner House (1803), 2520 East Franklin Street; Hilary Baker House (1810), 2302 East Grace Street; Ann Carrington House (1810), 2306 East Grace Street; Carrington Row (1818), 2307-11 East Broad Street; the Morris Cottages (1830-35), 25th and Grace Streets; Hardgrove House (1849), 2300 East Grace Street; and the Harwood and Estes Houses (1869), 2308-10 East Grace Street. The Hardgrove House is possibly the most interesting of these with its splendid Greek Revival portico and its amply proportioned rooms.

The Garden Club of Virginia has established a mews in the 2300 block, where many examples of 19th century Richmond cast iron have been installed. It should not be missed by the visitor with an interest in the subject.

A11   **City Hall** *1887-1894   Broad and 10th Sts.   Office hours*

Born of controversy, this magnificent Gothic Revival civic building has been returned to its original sparkle by being cleaned. It was designed by Elijah E. Myers, the architect of the state capitols of Utah, Michigan, Colorado, Texas and Idaho, and of the Parliament Buildings of Rio de Janeiro, but he was not called in until almost two decades after the earlier city hall had been torn down. Myers said of this building that "dignity of appearance is demanded by (its) uses," while others called it "a gem of architecture" and "evidence of Richmond's progress, prosperity, growth and ambition." One feature of the building which adds to the "dignity" is the breath-taking central hall, many stories high, surely as impressive a public interior as any in the country.

A12   **Confederate Museum** *1816-1818; c. 1852   1201 E. Clay St. Mon.-Sat. 9-5, Sun. 2-5   Fee*

When this house was built for John Brockenbrough, it had only two stories, the third being added about mid-century. It then served between 1861 and 1865 as the executive mansion for Jefferson Davis, President of the Confederacy, and in 1896 became the Confederate Museum. Its plan is unusual in that the three main rooms are *en suite* across the back of the house, while the staircase is at the side of the central entrance vestibule. This is a splendid solution for the city house, gaining privacy for the family and taking advantage of the garden. The marble mantels are especially noteworthy, and the portico on the garden side

A13

A14

A15

A16

shows the designer's personal variation on a classic order. The addition of the third story upsets the neo-classic proportions of the original and makes the building look more Victorian than it should.

A13 **Crozet House** *1814-1815; 1940* *100 E. Main St.* *Office hours*

One would suspect that the brick enframement of the door is a little early for the 19th century date, although the house itself, restored in 1940, conforms to the Federal style, which, in turn, was beginning to lose strength at that time. Lived in by Claudius Crozet for a few years after 1828, the house was built for Curtis Carter. Its interior woodwork has survived well even though at one time it was divided into a double house. It shows, too, that its urban situation directly on the sidewalk may be both pleasant and charming. It is occupied by the architectural firm of Marcellus Wright & Partners.

A14 **Diggs-Bullock-Christian House** *c. 1809; c. 1858; 1960* *204 W. Franklin St.* *By appointment*

This house, built by Cole Diggs c. 1809, was Victorianized c. 1858, when its porch, which had been on the east, was moved to the south and coarsened with "modern" detail, and when the house was stuccoed. A glimpse of the original building may be seen at the present rear, where the stucco was omitted and the keystones appear. A good bit of the delicate interior woodwork remains, and the present owner, Tucker Hospital, Inc., tried in its 1960 conversion of the building to retain as much of the original character as possible.

A15 **Egyptian Building** *1845* *College and Marshall Sts.* *College hours*

This first building put up especially for the Medical College of Virginia must have been both a shock and a surprise to Richmonders, for its Egyptian forms, carried out so precisely and so carefully, were very much against the current tradition in the city. Nevertheless it has survived with few exterior changes to become the finest Egyptian Revival building in the nation. Thomas Stewart, the architect, achieved a marvelously unified composition in this monumental and rather exotic manner. Even the fence has become a part of the design with its posts in the form of abstract mummies, their feet projecting for stability at the bottom.

A16 **First Federal Savings and Loan Association** *1964* *224 E. Broad St.* *Banking hours*

The designers of the First Federal Savings and Loan Association (the Cunneen Co. for the building and Herbert Uhl for the interiors) have combined the old banking house architectural virtues of solidity and dignity with a thoroughly contemporary spirit and form. The rich materials of rosewood, walnut and marble and the blockiness of the fire stair enclosure and that of the vault are reminiscent of the strength and luxury of older banking buildings, while the lightness of the glass of the upper

A17

A18

A19

A20

floors and the spatial treatment of the banking room proclaim this a modern building. The vault, quite properly, becomes the dominant feature of the interior and is as carefully designed as the other details. Of all the surprising features of this sensitive building, with its principal entrance on the parking lot rather than on one of the streets, the most surprising is the inclusion of a heliport on the roof.

A17 **Glasgow House** *1841; later additions*   *1 W. Main St.*   *Private*

David M. Branch built this Greek Revival house in 1841, but the wing was added at an undetermined date. Its Doric portico, its beautiful iron fence and its well-preserved interiors make it one of the more important of Richmond's Greek Revival houses. The Glasgow family held it from 1887 until 1945, when it was purchased by the Association for the Preservation of Virginia Antiquities. It is now leased by the Richmond Area University Center.

A18 **Governor's Mansion** *1811-13; 1865; 1908; 1955; 1956*   *Capitol Square*   *Open during Garden Week*

Built to replace an earlier wooden Governor's Mansion on the same site, the present one has been continuously occupied by Virginia's Governors, and has been almost as continuously remodeled. The balustrades between the chimneys and around the porch roofs were removed after 1865; a magnificent dining room designed by Duncan Lee was added at the rear in 1908; in 1955, the present brick wall replaced the pre-1860 iron fence; and in 1956 a balustrade was again placed between the chimneys. In spite of all these changes, the original woodwork may still be seen in the two front rooms, while the approach side of the mansion still retains a major portion of its early classicism.

A19 **Grant Tobacco Factory** *1853; later addition*   *1900 E. Franklin St. Private*

One of the few factory buildings to have survived from the mid-19th century, the Grant Tobacco Co. was designed by Samuel Freeman of Richmond, a fact recorded on a plaque in the gable. His plain but well-porportioned building with its stepped gables is both functional and human in scale. The later addition on 19th Street detracts somewhat from the effect of the original. Freeman put up the building for William H. Grant, but it is now owned by M. F. Neale and Co.

A20 **Hancock-Caskie House** *1808-09; c. 1852*   *2 N. 5th St.*   *Office hours or by appointment*

When Michael Hancock put up this house it was one of several similarly shaped houses in Richmond, with three-sided bays and two-story porch between. It is now the last of these to survive. The major change in the house seems to be the use of the Victorian mantels and the later, but handsome, iron fence. The architectonic scheme of the porch, the splendid lintels and keystones of the windows, and the fine interior woodwork, es-

A21

A22

A23

32   Architecture in Virginia

pecially in the octagonal living room, mark this house as a most superior example of a now almost vanished type. It is presently owned by the American Red Cross.

A21 **Hollywood Cemetery** *1847   412 S. Cherry St.   Spring, summer, 7:30-6; fall, winter, -5*

Hollywood Cemetery was the first private cemetery in Richmond. The land was purchased by 25 gentlemen, but a stock company was formed on August 3, 1847. It was begun, curiously enough, over strong objections, but became popular after 1856. First named Mt. Vernon, it became Hollywood in 1848 because of the admiration its second and principal designer had for its holly trees.

The cemetery was first laid out by a Mr. Pratt, but the directors asked John Notman to give them "a more complete and precise plan than that which had been submitted by Mr. Pratt." Notman, a Scotsman trained in Edinburgh, had settled in Philadelphia in 1834 and had worked on Laurel Hill Cemetery there in 1836. At Hollywood he utilized the magnificent site in a most picturesque way, achieving a great variety of views with his planning of the roads, which follow the contours of the hilly land wherever possible.

There are two remarkable monuments in the cemetery. The earlier is the cast iron tomb of Monroe, whose body was moved here during the centennial of his birth (1858). It was designed by a Richmond architect, Albert Lybrock, and cast in Philadelphia by Wood and Perot. The other monument, a tour de force of construction, is the dry stone pyramid set up to memorialize the Confederate dead.

Notman's cemetery, with its views over the city, its elaborate iron fences, its winding roads, its lush foliage and its monuments (among which the obelisk is so frequently repeated) is one of the best of the designs of the picturesque school left in the Commonwealth.

A22 **Iron Fronts** *c. 1865   1207-1211 E. Main St.*

After the Evacuation Fire of the Civil War, there was a great need for business buildings in Richmond. The builders made lavish use of iron, both because of safety and of fashion, and East Main from 9th to 15th Streets was lined with iron-fronted or iron-decorated business blocks. Of the survivors, that at 1207-1211 is a fine example, its four stories richly decorated in an Italianate manner with pilasters, balusters, arches, brackets and entablatures. This particular group was cast in Baltimore by the firm of Hayward Bartlett, but many of these fronts were cast in Richmond. The buildings are owned by Morris A. Bloom and Hyman Specter.

A23 **Ironwork** *c. 1850   1012 E. Marshall St.*

Richmond is an outdoor museum of cast iron, and it is impossible to list all the sites worthy of attention. From the casting of the first railings in 1817 until the 1890's, cast iron was used in the city almost as a matter of course. Perhaps the most typical,

A24

A25

A26

34 Architecture in Virginia

and one of the most beautiful, mid-19th century examples is the two story porch of the Putney house at 1012 East Marshall Street. It was cast by the Phoenix Iron Works, owned by William B. Cook, who made good use of the strength, as well as the laciness, inherent in the material.

There are many other examples of cast iron and many other stylistic expressions to be seen along the streets of the city. The interested visitor is advised to be sharp-eyed.

A24 **Jefferson Hotel** *1893-95; 1901*   *116 W. Main St.*

When Major Lewis Ginter commissioned the firm of Carrère and Hastings to build the Jefferson Hotel in Richmond, he told them that he wanted the finest hostelry in the South. This they achieved, working with freedom and enthusiasm in their personal Edwardian, eclectic manner.

Some may wonder why the architects chose a Mediterranean style for an area steeped in the classical tradition, but such was the spirit of the time. When the Jefferson was finished it was among the most luxurious hotels in America. Constructed on two levels because of its sloping site, the hotel afforded interlocking vistas a block deep, giving the public rooms a grandeur that almost suggests Piranesi's drawings. The best in fabrics, china and crystal were brought from Europe to furnish the interior, and contemporary works of painting and sculpture were installed to provide final touches of elegance.

Much altered by rebuilding after fire damage, its grand axis now divided and closed off, the Jefferson still retains an air of quality, derived from the distinction of its original conception.

A25 **Library, Virginia Union University** *1939*   *Lombardy St. and Brook Rd.*   *University hours*

Designed by Victor Bourgeois and Leo Stijnen, under the direction of Professor Henry van der Velde (the most important Belgian architect of the 20th century and the predecessor of Walter Gropius as head of what was then the Grand Ducal School of Art at Weimar), this building was first constructed as the Belgian Pavilion at the New York World's Fair in 1939. It had been intended to return the building to Belgium for use at one of her universities, but, World War II intervening, the Belgian ambassador gave it to Virginia Union University. It was dismantled in New York, shipped to Richmond, and reassembled on its present site, where it has become a monument of the modernism of the thirties. It is worth mentioning, too, that its materials are symbolic, representing the national unity of Belgium in its use of the red tiles of Flanders, the black slate of the Ardennes, and the plate glass of the Walloon areas.

A26 **Life of Virginia Building** *1965*   *910 Capitol St.*   *By appointment, Public Relations Department*

Because it is attached to an existing structure, the new Life of Virginia building gained an advantage tall buildings seldom use today. The old building had stories of different heights that

A27

A28

A29

were carried into the new structure because their floors are connected. This variation in height results in a vivacity of proportion almost never seen in today's multi-floored buildings. The firmness of modeling of the corners, the rhythm of the window divisions and the strong structural elements combined with the very clear plan more than justify the awards already won by this thoughtful commercial building. Commissioned most intelligently by the Life Insurance Company of Virginia, it was designed by Marcellus Wright and Partners.

A27 **Linden Row** *1847; 1853   100-118 E. Franklin St.   Shops, business hours*

Fleming James built the first five of the houses in Linden Row, and in 1853 the western end of the block was completed after the same design by Samuel and Alexander Rutherfoord. Unfortunately, the two units on the east were demolished in 1922, but the eight remaining units in this block give a wonderful picture of the effect of an expanse of Greek Revival row houses.

The granite retaining walls at the street, the iron fences, the sturdy porticoes, the expansiveness of the glass areas and crispness of the white trim against the brick make a city scene of great distinction. Miss Mary Wingfield Scott owns seven of the units today, and the Val-Gase Studio owns the eighth.

A28 **Main Street Station** *1901   1520 E. Main St.*

In 1901, Wilson, Harris and Richards of Philadelphia erected this excellent example of the extreme romanticism that flourished during the period of the eclectic revivals. Here we have an adaption of the French Renaissance style, established and fostered in America by Richard Morris Hunt, who had trained at the Beaux Arts in Paris. The steep roofs and numerous dormers are also hallmarks of the medievalism introduced in England in the 1840's by John Ruskin and his circle.

The station in Richmond still boasts its spacious cast-iron shed, one of the few remaining examples in this country of a form developed out of a new material for a new purpose. Trustees of the station are Chesapeake & Ohio Railway Company and Seaboard Coast Line Railroad Company.

A29 **Marshall House** *1788-91; c. 1810   Marshall and 9th Sts.   Mon.-Sat., 10-5; Sun., 2-5   Fee*

When John Marshall moved to Richmond, he lived in a wooden house until his new brick house was built. By 1810 the small wing had been added, and the three porches were also in existence, according to an insurance policy of the time. The house stood in an entire block, with wooden outbuildings consisting of an office, a kitchen, a laundry and the stables. The city, of course, encroached on this land, to the point that in 1907 a councilman declared the house would spoil a new school that was being built on the block. But a group of women's organizations saved it, and the house now is the only surviving 18th century brick house in Richmond. It has even survived the school, and once more sits in a large lot, thanks to urban renewal.

A30

A31

A32

38   Architecture in Virginia

Though of so late a date, the building is a rather noncommittal version of Georgian on the exterior. Its first-floor interiors are more elaborate, with especially fine paneling in the library and parlor. Mantels and cornices are notable. Richmond still owns the house, but it is maintained and operated by the Association for the Preservation of Virginia Antiquities.

A30 **Model Tobacco Building** *1938-40   1100 Jefferson Davis Hwy. Private*

The Model Tobacco Factory, designed by the Chicago architects Schmidt, Garden and Erikson, is an excellent example of the abandonment of both the romantic and the *laissez-faire* attitudes of factory owners toward the design of their industrial structures; that is, no effort was made to give it a false nobility, nor was it allowed simply to "happen." Instead, great care was taken to make it handsome and to allow it to express both its purpose and its contemporaneity. Once more the choice of materials plays its part, and one sees materials unknown before the 20th century being used with great effect.

The horizontality of the massed windows at the sides, contrasted with the vertical elements of the entrance feature, the architectural function of the sign and the related design of the gate posts, all combine to give the building its 20th century air and its distinction.

A31 **Monument Avenue** *1906   West from Lombardy St.*

The addition of the monument to J. E. B. Stuart (1907) to those of Robert E. Lee (1890) and Jefferson Davis (1907) on Franklin Street is credited with having given the city fathers the idea of widening the street to 130 feet, extending it, and renaming it Monument Avenue. The action was promptly approved, and the first paving was done in 1907. By 1915 the street had been extended some five miles to Horsepen Road, and a monument to Thomas J. "Stonewall" Jackson was added in 1919, while another to Matthew Fontaine Maury was put up in 1929. The street's central strip of grass, its four rows of trees and its handsome residences combine to make of it one of the finest streets not only in Richmond but in the nation. It has not, fortunately, lost its character, although some of its residences have become offices. It is, indeed, a supreme example of the unifying power of space, scale and trees on the urban scene.

A32 **Monumental Church** *1812-14   1224 E. Broad St.   Mon.-Fri., 9-4*

On December 26, 1811, a theatre on this site burned, with the loss of over 70 lives. Richmonders decided to memorialize this national tragedy by building a church over the former theatre, with the fire's victims entombed beneath the nave. The commission was given to Robert Mills, who produced a version of his auditorium-type church with a shallow dome surmounted by a low lantern. Its large portico housed the actual monument to the dead. In 1814 the church had a dignity no other church in Richmond possessed. The octagonal church just misses being a tremendous success, for there are a few awkward proportions and uses of orders in it. It is now owned by the Medical College

A33

A34

A35

A36

of Virginia, which uses it as a student chapel in accordance with the original directive that it should be "a Monumental Church to be forever kept sacred for the purpose of divine worship."

A33 **Morson's Row** *1853   219-223 Governor St.   Private*

Richmond was still building the Greek Revival Linden Row when these Victorian row houses were erected by James Marion Morson. The bow fronts, which helped to increase the light and the view; the balconied, arched door enframements; the heavy, bracketed cornices; and the elaborately molded, consoled lintels over the windows—all mark the break with the earlier style. These charming houses still retain their mahogany doors and marble mantels. Because they add an immense amount of verve and variety to the environs of the Capitol, they should be retained in the new development for State office buildings.

A34 **Old First Baptist Church** *1841; 1858; 1868; 1938-39   Broad and 12th Sts.   Public restaurant*

This beautiful Greek Doric building, designed by Thomas U. Walter of Philadelphia, has survived only by being radically changed in purpose, for it has been since 1938-39 the student center for the Medical College of Virginia. It was expanded in 1858 by an addition at the rear; it was altered in 1868; the side chapel was added in 1870; and its wooden belfry was removed in 1938. Walter's magnificent columns in antis, deep-set entrance porch and coupled pilasters create an effect of strong contrasts, particularly welcome today when the building is surrounded by rather more bland designs. The congregation of this church liked the entrance feature so well that a similar one was designed for its new and considerably larger building.

A35 **Philip Morris Operations Center** *1964   4001 Commerce Rd.; Bells Road exit off Interstate 95   By appointment*

Ulrich Franzen and Associates designed the center for Philip Morris, Inc., to house high-level management, and its plan is a model of coordinating the interacting flow of the various divisions of a business. One of the major 20th century contributions to architecture is the new importance given to industrial buildings, and this center at Philip Morris is an excellent example of the new expression.

A36 **Reed House** *1927   River Rd.   Private*

Set among old trees that had been planted for an earlier house, Redesdale, as this house is sometimes called, was designed by William Lawrence Bottomley to take advantage of its views of the James River. Consequently its living room and dining room are on that side, and the architect, within the neo-Georgianism of the period between the World Wars, created a nostalgic and inspired, but not an imitative house. Working at a scale as large or larger than that of the Tidewater houses of the 18th century, he created a new harmony of mass, proportion and delicacy of detail. The house is owned by Mrs. Leslie H. Reed.

A37

A38

A39

A40

42   Architecture in Virginia

A37 **Reynolds Metals Building** *1958   6601 W. Broad St.   Office hours*

The Reynolds Metals Building represents one school of contemporary design in which the classical elements of symmetry, the courtyard, the podium and the peristyle are employed. The dramatic use of glass, the flat roof, the sun-moved vertical louvers and the modular system of construction are all characteristic of fine modern architecture. The exterior metal facing of the building is entirely in weatherproof aluminum, which perhaps will be the metal of experiment of the 20th century as cast iron was of the 19th.

The building has been thoughtfully located on a large, partially wooded plot near the outskirts of Richmond, with ample parking for workers and visitors. Handsome landscaping relates the structure to its site, and preserves and emphasizes the beauties of sunlight, water, greenery and open air.

The rich brick paving in the courtyard has been carried through into the reception lobby. The interior furnishings, including the works of art, are in harmony with the entire scheme, as designed by Skidmore, Owings and Merrill.

A38 **Rice House** *1964   Lock Island, 1000 Old Lock Lane   Private*

Designed by Richard Neutra, this house is an exposition of his theme of bringing nature into the home by the use of floor to ceiling windows, fourteen sliding glass doors, a mirrored stair wall that reflects the view and an alliance with the natural forms, such as the granite boulders, which may be found on the site. The island was, of course, chosen for its spectacular views, which are of a sort almost never found within a city. The geometry of the house and the prodigality of nature achieve a most harmonious union here. The house was built for Mr. and Mrs. Walter L. Rice.

A39 **St. Paul's Episcopal Church** *1844-45   815 E. Grace St.; Mon-Sat., 10-4; guided tours after Sunday service, 1-4*

Designed by Thomas S. Stewart of Philadelphia, St. Paul's Church is one of the best examples of the Greek Revival in Richmond. Its Corinthian columns are superbly detailed. Its ceiling, with the great, gold central panel in plaster relief, is most unusual. Although it has lost its steeple, its tower shows an interesting combination of strength and lightness. And its beautiful fence, cast in Richmond, has survived with no more than the needless loss of its original gas lamps, though most of its many Greek allusions are still in place. The interior has a baptismal font (1857-59) carved by the Virginia sculptor Alexander Galt, and at least one Tiffany window (1898), designed by Frederick Wilson and dedicated to Jefferson Davis.

A40 **Shockoe Slip Area** *19th century   near 13th St., south of Cary St.*

Though dilapidated, the Shockoe Slip area in Richmond is one of the few remaining open bits of 19th century cityscape. Its variety of materials—cobblestone paving, brick or stone sidewalks, the cannon used as bollards, the carved stone of the

A41

A42

A43

A44

44   Architecture in Virginia

fountain for horses, the brick, stucco and iron of the buildings—and its buildings, which still retain a human scale, demonstrate the amenities possible before gigantism dominated business. Tobacco and cotton warehouses, the Tobacco Exchange and even a hotel were here, the hotel having been replaced in 1871 by the offices contained in the Columbian Block, still standing.

A41 **State Planters Bank** *1960 1801 W. Broad St. Banking hours*

In 1962 this branch bank was awarded the First Honor Award for excellence in design by the Virginia Chapter of the American Institute of Architects. One can well understand this award to its architects, Rawlings and Wilson, for the reticence of the building, its careful detail, its studied proportion and its welcoming courtyard make of it an unusually complete design. Its effect has been somewhat marred, unfortunately, by the later addition of the sign.

A42 **United States Post Office** *1855-59; 1889; 1910-12; 1930-32 10th and Main Sts. Business hours*

This superb granite building has miraculously retained its original character throughout its many additions, for the architects following Ammi B. Young, who designed it originally, wisely worked in sympathy with Young's Italianate scheme. At first the building was a long, narrow rectangle the width, on Main Street, of the five central arches; short wings were added on either side of this block at the front and back in 1889; in 1910, the building was extended to Tenth Street, and another story was added; and in 1930 it was extended to the east. Though the federal government threatens from time to time to abandon this building, Richmond should not allow it to be demolished, for its strong Victorianism is a happy focal point in the city's business district.

A43 **Virginia House** *1925-28 4301 Sulgrave Rd. Tues.-Sat., 10-4; Sun., 2-5 Fee*

Designed by Henry Grant Morse, Virginia House incorporates portions of the 16th century English house Warwick Priory. Much of the stone in the exterior walls and parts of the interior woodwork, including the stair, are original. In addition, the tower is a reproduction of one at Wormeleighton in England, and the wing to the west of the main entrance door is based on Sulgrave Manor, the ancestral Washington home. The house and its extensive and elaborate gardens were given to the Virginia Historical Society in 1929 by the original owners, Mr. and Mrs. Alexander W. Weddell, who felt the Society should have a Tudor house. Virginia House is now maintained by the Society, and it serves not only as a reminiscence of Tudor England, but also of the expansiveness possible during the eclecticism of the 1920's.

A44 **Whitlock-Graham House** *1883 201 W. Franklin St. Office hours*

Robert H. Whitlock built this elaborate house in 1883. Its successful combination of French Renaissance elements with the

A45

A45

A46

spiky, angular type of floral ornamentation now generally classified as Eastlake make of it an absorbing study in High Victorianism. Owned at present by W. Randolph Graham, M.D., who has transformed it into offices and apartments, it has, nevertheless, survived without much change. Beautiful materials and careful detail were lavished on the house originally and have proved their worth by their present utility and condition. Notice especially the iron fence, which brought Richmond's cast iron tradition up-to-date as of 1883, the carved granite gate and fence posts, the marble walk to the house, the fireplaces with their brass hoods and encaustic tile hearths and the carved panels of the outer doors.

A45 **Wickham-Valentine House** *1812; c. 1850   1015 E. Clay St. Mon.-Sat., 10-5; Sun., 2:30-5   Fee*

Attributed to Robert Mills, this beautiful Federal house depends for its exterior effect on proportion and for its interior effect on the lightness, delicacy and invention of its trim. Its variety of shaped rooms and its principal stair, both cantilevered and spiral, almost free-form in plan, give unusual distinction to the house. In the 1850's it was modernized in the Victorian taste, and when it was restored the drawing room was wisely left as a Victorian monument, although it is still possible to see most of the original 1812 room under the mid-19th century overlay. The Wickham-Valentine house is now a part of the Valentine Museum of the Life and History of Richmond.

A46 **Wilton** *1750-53; 1933-35   South Wilton Road: drive west on Main Street, following Route 147; at the end of the 5300 block on Cary Street Road turn left on South Wilton Road, which ends at Wilton   Weekdays, 10-5; Sun. (Labor Day to July 1 only), 3-5*

Wilton was built for William Randolph, III, on a high bluff overlooking the James River some fifteen miles from its present site. There were two offices, a storehouse, a dairy and a kitchen as outbuildings at the original plantation. Always a well-known house but frequently neglected, it was described by a visitor in 1833: "but such ruin! Broken down fences, a falling piazza, defaced paint, banisters tied up with ropes etc., etc. . . . ."

In 1933 the Colonial Dames took title to Wilton, moved it to its new but similar site, and lovingly restored and furnished it. Its exterior has some of the best domestic brickwork in the state, while its interior is the only one in the country to be paneled from floor to ceiling in every room, hall and alcove. It is impossible to understand the mid-Georgian movement in Virginia without knowing Wilton.

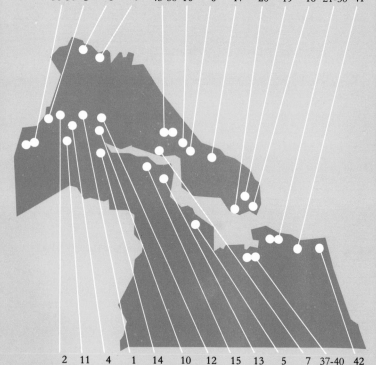

The tidewater region of Virginia presented to the first colonists an abundance of timber and clay for building purposes, and by this means the brick and wood tradition of Virginia came into being. But the hot, humid climate also offered a terrible contrast to the cool English homeland, and soon taught the colonists the virtues of chimneys on the outside walls for the dispersion of heat, center halls for cool drafts, high ceilings and detached kitchens (when possible), a pattern that continued until the coming of mechanical climate control.

The rivers of this region served as the early highways for the plantations, the houses of which frequently had their principal entrance turned to the river rather than the land. The roads were secondary; in fact, the "crossroads," a term recurring in many Virginia place names, was just that—a place where the roads between plantations crossed, sometimes serving as the convenient site for a church, an inn, a courthouse and a post office.

This area, of course, being the first to develop, included many of the early and most important of Virginia's buildings.

Yorktown in 1755

B1

B2

B3

B4

50 Architecture in Virginia

B₁   **Belle Air** *c. 1670; late 18th century; 1880; 1950   Charles City Co.* (¼ *mile east of Charles City on Route 5*) *Mon.-Sat., 9-5; Sun., by appt.   Fee*

Although Belle Air began as a jerkin-headed or clipped-gable roofed house built (probably for Lt. Col. Daniel Clarke) in the 17th century, it was extended, transoms were placed over the doors, and the roof was given its present form in the late 18th century. A detached kitchen was built in 1880 and connected to the present house in 1950. Long neglected, the restoration of Belle Air was begun in 1950. The interior has retained some of its exposed 17th century framing of heart pine, and its 17th century staircase, also of pine, is fortunately intact. Its strong balusters and closed stringer contrast with 18th century examples. The present owners are Mr. and Mrs. Walter O. Major.

B₂   **Berkeley** *1726; c. 1790; 1926   Charles City Co.* (26 *miles east of Richmond on Route 5*) *Private*

When the present owners, Mr. and Mrs. Malcolm Jamieson, purchased Berkeley in 1926, there was a porch on all four sides of the house. They removed the porch and roofed the basement entrance at that time. The original builder, Benjamin Harrison IV, had been forward looking in his use of the heroic pediment roof, the first in Virginia. Benjamin Harrison VI removed the original paneling c. 1790 and installed the simpler paneling then fashionable. The walls of this sturdy mansion, floored with hand-hewn heart pine, are three feet thick.

B₃   **Shirley** *c. 1740; c. 1769; c. 1831   Charles City Co.* (25 *miles east of Richmond on Route 5*) *Daily except Christmas   Fee*

The dating problems at Shirley are vexing, and only approximate dates may be fixed. The dependencies of the forecourt are probably from c. 1740, and certainly the steep, pedimented roofs on two of them, similar to the roof at Berkeley, would tend to confirm this date. The house itself was finished by 1769 or 1770, but the date of the present porches is now thought to be 1831, as three new porches are mentioned in a painter's bill of that year. Recent investigation has shown, too, that there are brick supports for from two to five prior porches under the floor of the present rear porch.

    Whatever the exact dates for the various structures at Shirley, this plantation complex forms one of the most interesting in the State. The two-story porches of the main house, its extraordinary roof topped with a pineapple finial, its suspended stair, its rich interior paneling, and its plan (which lacks the usual center hall) all mark it as unique. It is still owned and operated as a plantation by descendants of the original builders, Mr. and Mrs. Charles Hill Carter, Jr.

B₄   **Westover** *c. 1730; 1900-05   Charles City Co.* (28 *miles east of Richmond on Route 5*) *Gardens and grounds only 9-5   Fee*

In 1729 William Byrd, II, wrote, "In a year or 2 I intend to set about building a very good house." He had already, probably in 1711, set up the beautiful iron gates, which were unique

B5

B6

B6

in the colony, and which survive. The two dependencies were originally detached from the house, but in 1900-05 the connecting units were built, and the east dependency, which had been burned in the Civil War, was restored. The central house, with its steep roof, its hipped dormers, its door enframements and its segment-headed windows is the very apogee of the early Georgian period in Virginia.

There is a puzzle about the date of the interiors at Westover. A notice in the *Virginia Gazette* states that on January 7, 1748 (old style), Westover was "burned to the ground, with the loss of all the furniture, clothes, plate, liquore." The rococo plaster work of the ceilings might bear this out, but the paneling and the mantels are of early rather than mid-18th century design. Either the report was exaggerated or the interior was recopied largely in its original form. As of today, the major change of the interior is the throwing together of two rooms to make the present dining room. The house is now owned by Mrs. Bruce Crane Fisher.

B5 **St. Luke's Church** *16-?; 1887-94; 1953-57   Isle of Wight Co. (On Route 10 at Benn's Church, 4 miles east of Smithfield) 9-5*

In the absence of documents there is great uncertainty about the date of St. Luke's Church. One authority gives 1632 (though this is very dubious), another 1682, and a third c. 1665. Whatever the date, St. Luke's is the only *original* Gothic building to have survived in the nation, and, as such, becomes doubly precious both for its own architectural values and for its unique importance as a true Gothic structure. The roof and part of the east gable were blown down in 1887, and the structure was carefully restored in 1953-57. The only original interior woodwork is the architrave over the principal door, a single baluster (second from the left) in the altar rail and the sounding board over the pulpit. The brick tracery, the buttresses, the stepped gables, and the tower are all, though frequently repaired, in their original form. It has been pointed out that the round windows in the tower and the curious pediment over its entrace are harbingers of the classicism that swept away the Gothic outlook so strongly seen in this church.

B6 **Carter's Grove** *1750-55; 1927-28   James City Co. (Route 60, 6 miles east of Williamsburg) March 1 to Thanksgiving, 10-5   Fee*

Built for Carter Burwell by David Minitree (the original accounts have survived) Carter's Grove was first a central house with two detached dependencies probably of a slightly earlier date. It sat, as it still does, on a height above the James River. The river façade is just as important as the land façade, and the great terraces leading to the river, so important as a means of transportation, are still in place. In 1927-28, the roof of the main house was raised, dormers were introduced, and units connecting the central house with its dependencies were built. The building was thus given an exterior aspect of some twenty-five years before its actual date.

Inside, however, its magnificent paneling was carefully put into condition once more. Its great glory is its central hall, which

B7

B7

B8

carries a splendid stair at the land side and widens into a most architectural (pedestaled pilasters and full entablature) yet hospitable room on the water side.

Whatever the discrepancies of the 1927-28 alterations, this extraordinary and original interior will always make Carter's Grove unique. The house is now owned by the Seatlantic Fund, Inc.

B7   **Jamestown** *1607-98   James City Co.*

Jamestown, as the first permanent settlement in Virginia, was bound to have a difficult time architecturally. Indeed, there always seems to have been an air, sometimes greater than others, of improvisation about its buildings. Whatever the first settlers may have been, they do not seem to have been very expert builders. Captain John Smith had to show them how to keep their roofs and windows from leaking. He called the 1607 church a "miserable hovel" and a "homely thing like a barne, set upon cratchets, covered with raftes, sedge, and earth." This structure was replaced in 1608, again in 1610; needing repairs in 1611, the 1610 church was not replaced until 1617. That building, in turn, needed repairs in 1619 and 1624, and perhaps in 1636. Between 1639 and 1644 a brick church was built, and a tower, the present ruin, added in 1647. The church behind the present tower was put up in 1907, and it and the tower are now owned and maintained by the Association for the Preservation of Virginia Antiquities.

Fire was a great enemy of Jamestown, built largely of thatch, wattle and daub, or timber (as is the reconstruction of the first glass factory) or "raftes, sedge, and earth" as Captain John Smith said. And it was fire that eventually drove the government to Middle Plantation. As early as 1722 the town was in ruins. Hugh Jones said that year that "the first metropolis, James Town, was built in the most convenient place for trade and security against the Indians, but often received much damage, being twice burnt down; after which it never recovered its perfection, consisting at present of nothing but abundance of brick rubbish, and three or four good inhabited houses . . . " By 1777 its condition was apparently worse, for it was described as being "interesting only from its early associations and venerable ruins."

Unfortunately, the "venerable ruins" are too sparse for any accurate idea of the appearance of the town in the 17th century to be formed. But as the earliest of the English-speaking settlements on this continent, it has an archaeological interest which makes up for the lack of architectural information to be gained by a visit there.

B8   **Hampstead** *c. 1825   New Kent Co. (From Richmond, north 13 miles on Route 360, east on Route 606 for 9 miles to brick gateposts on right) Private*

This neo-classic house, built for Conrad Webb, is still in very close to its original condition. Its elongated portico with its narrow intercolumniation, the uncopied capitals of its columns, its elaborate entablature, its extraordinary parapet hiding the

B9

B10

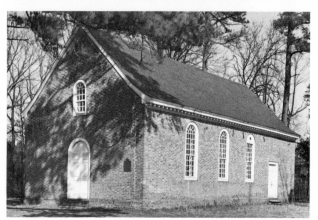

B11

56 Architecture in Virginia

low-pitched roof and pierced with guilloche panels, and its captain's walk, all slightly provincial in execution and proportion, are matched and even surpassed by the free-standing spiral staircase of the interior. Among the outbuildings were an ice house, which survives, and a granary, which burned in 1965. It is now owned by Mrs. William J. Wallace, Sr.

B9 **St. Peter's Church** *1701-03; c. 1740; 1950-51 New Kent Co. (North at Talleysville from Route 33 to Route 609 for 1 mile, then right at sign on Route 642 to church)*

Still in an isolated and rural area, St. Peter's Church was first built in 1701-03, replacing an earlier church, which was at an unknown location. Its tower was added, presumably in stages, c. 1740. It has had many additions, repairs and restorations in both the 19th and 20th centuries, so that its original work is to be found primarily in its walls. One authority describes it and Yeocomico church as representing "the transition in Virginia's ecclesiastical buildings from late Gothic to Classical. This claim for St. Peter's may be noted principally by the restored strapwork and the double casement windows on the one hand and by the original chancel window and the differences in the two storeys of the tower on the other hand."

The precise form, then, of the Flemish gables, the casement windows and even the steeple of the tower is conjectural, based on the practices of the time and some, but not complete, archaeological evidence. What is original, and interesting, about the tower is the use of one of the stuccoed urns at the corners as a chimney for the corner fireplace of the room over the porch, as well as the oak gutters that project over the north and south windows, presumably draining such rain as entered the steeple through the louvered dormers.

B10 **Brandon** *c. 1765; 19th century   Prince George Co. (At Burrowsville, east of Hopewell on Route 10, turn east on Route 611 for 6 miles) Gardens only, 9-5:30   Fee*

Though the land grant at Brandon is a very early one, there does not seem to have been a mansion there until after the marriage of Nathaniel Harrison in 1765. Two earlier houses, which had been built in a straight line, became the wings for a central block and connecting units. This five-part plan is very similar to a plate in Robert Morris' *Select Architecture*, 1755. The house is often attributed to Jefferson, but the attribution is not yet certain, though it is known that Jefferson owned a copy of Morris' book. In the 19th century, the two porches were substituted for earlier ones, but the interior paneling, though suffering during the Civil War, is largely intact. The house is presently owned by Mrs. Robert W. Daniel.

B11 **Merchant's Hope Church** *1657 (?) Prince George Co. (From Hopewell 4 miles east on Route 10, turn right on Route 641) Open during services*

1657 is cut into one of the large and original beams of this early ecclesiastical building. Although some authorities dispute this

B12

B13

B14

58 Architecture in Virginia

date, the most recent accepts it and says that it is supported by the utter simplicity of the west doorway and the Tudor swag or kick of the roof at the eaves. The walls have not had, nor have they needed, much repair, and the original stone paving of the aisles is still in place. The present doors and window sash are probably colonial, though not necessarily original. It is thought that Merchant's Hope is the state's oldest surviving church, and it is sad to have to record that it was not used for services from the time of the Disestablishment after the Revolution until 1870.

B12 **Upper Brandon** *1820; c. 1850-70   Prince George Co. (Turn left at Burrowsville east of Hopewell from Route 10 to Route 611 for 1 mile, turn left on Route 653 for 5½ miles, follow signs) Private*

Built first by William Byrd Harrison for his son, Upper Brandon is a fine example of the amplitude which could be expressed through the proportions and simplified detail of the Federal style. The kitchen and schoolhouse dependencies were originally separate from the main house. Sometime between 1850 and 1870 the already large main house was enlarged by the addition of the two wings, and the two dependencies were connected to it by semi-underground passages. Upper Brandon is now the property of Mr. Fred E. Watkins.

B13 **Bacon's Castle** *c. 1655-70; 1810-20; 1942   Surry Co. (From the town of Bacon's Castle on Route 10, northeast on Route 617 to house on left) Private*

Built for Arthur Allen sometime after 1655, Bacon's Castle is the only "high" Jacobean house in this country. Its original plan is uncertain, but as the chamfered beams seem to run through the present partitions, there may have been one large room or two rooms and no hall on the first floor originally. The latter seems the more likely. The addition to the house was built in 1810-20 by William Hankins, and it is believed the paneling in the older portion of the house, though of the 17th century, is about 20 years later than the house itself. When the house was restored in 1942 by the present owners, Mr. and Mrs. Walker Pegram Warren, they were unable to replace the original, mullioned windows or the entrance. In spite of these anomalies, the shaped gables, the magnificent chimneys with their three, diagonally-set flues and the "porch" towers give a very clear idea of the Jacobean features of the house.

B14 **Claremont Manor** *c. 1650-60 (?); c. 1717; 1940; 1950-64   Surry Co. (From Surry 9 miles west on Route 10 to Spring Grove, north for 5 miles on Route 646, through Claremont to the manor gate) Private*

Legend and most uncertain dating surround Claremont Manor, the focal point of the small village of Claremont. A mid-17th century house was apparently built on the site for Arthur Allen. *Perhaps* portions of this earlier house were incorporated in the later house of c. 1717. One account states that the Manor was virtually razed during the Civil War. It is known that it was restored in 1940 by the architect William Lawrence Bottomley; changed by the next owner; and restored once more between

B15

B16

B17

1950 and 1964. Since 1964 it has belonged to the Felician Sisters, O. S. F. Although the T-shaped plan and the position of the ballroom make this a most unusual house, it is almost impossible to distinguish any of the original work under the many restorations.

B15 **Rolfe-Warren House** *1652; 1935   Surry Co. (Route 31 between Surry and Scotland Wharf) Apr. 1-Oct. 31, 9-5   Fee*

Though built on land presented in 1614 to John Rolfe by Chief Powhatan, the Rolfe-Warren house was apparently put up for or by Thomas Warren and was known as the "Fifty Foot Brick House." It is also sometimes known as Smith's Fort Plantation. Acquired by the Association for the Preservation of Virginia Antiquities in 1929, it was restored to its present condition in 1935, a condition that would appear to be more 18th century than 17th century.

B16 **Colonial Parkway** *c. 1938-40; c. 1957   York and James City Counties*

As early as 1909-11, York and James City Counties and the City of Williamsburg had broached the idea of a connecting road between the three national shrines. In 1930 enabling legislation for the parkway was introduced into Congress by Representative Louis C. Cramton of Michigan. Actual construction began in the late 1930's on the first section, while the final section was completed in 1957. The design, landscaping and construction of the parkway were under the joint direction of the National Park Service and the Bureau of Public Roads.

Just as the Skyline Drive, with its spectacular views over the mountains, is a triumph, so is the Colonial Parkway, with its very different topography. Gently rolling countryside combined with glimpses of the York or James Rivers and imaginative landscaping create serenely beautiful approaches to the shrines. It is, in fact, the result of the best efforts of collaboration, and shows that intelligence in government may lead to a masterpiece.

B17 **Yorktown** *York Co.*

Yorktown, a small village on the bluffs overlooking the York River, is a site of great natural interest, and has several architectural monuments that should be seen in any survey of Virginia architecture. It is also a town that has been singularly exposed to the vicissitudes of war, evidences of which may still be seen in several of its houses. On Tuesday, April 29, 1777, Nicholas Crosswell wrote in his journal that he "dined at Yorktown, 24 miles from Hampton. This is a pleasant town situated upon York River which is navigable for the largest ships. Close to the town there are several very good Gentlemen's houses built of brick and some of their gardens are laid out with the greatest taste of any I have seen in America, but now almost ruined by the disorderly soldiers, and, what is more extraordinary, their own soldiers the guardians of the people and the defenders of their rights. Houses burnt down, others pulled to pieces for fuel, most of the Gardens thrown to the street,

B17

B17

B18

62 Architecture in Virginia

everything in disorder and confusion and no appearance of trade. This melancholy scene fills the mind of the itinerant traveller with gloomy and horrid ideas. Here is a battery consisting of 12 pieces of heavy cannon to command the River and a company of artillery stationed here, but they make a sorry appearance for so respectable a corps, as the Artillery ought to be."

Grace Church (1697) is interesting not only for its age but also for its structure, which is a local material called marl. Marl is defined as "deposits of shells of various types mixed with muck and clay of the once ocean bottom." The lime in these "decomposing shells in composition with the clay" produces the "dense rocky substance known as marl." The church was apparently a simple rectangle at first, but was burned in 1814, not rebuilt until 1848, when it was stuccoed, and the present belfry was added in 1926.

The Nelson House (sometimes called York Hall) was built either by Thomas Nelson or his son William sometime between 1725 and 1740, probably nearer the latter date. This sturdy house, with its segmental headed windows, its quoins, its pedimented gables and strongly dentiled cornice, seems to have survived very well indeed the "disorder and confusion" of the various wars that have eddied about Yorktown. Its interior, with its central hall not quite on axis, is unchanged except for the balustrade of the staircase and perhaps the marble flooring of the hall. The paneling is among the most interesting in Virginia. Although there is a slight provincialism about the proportions of the Nelson house, its excellent preservation and its forthrightness give it a splendid independence. Mr. and Mrs. Anthony Blow now occupy the house.

The Moore house, built well before the surrender of Yorktown on October 15, 1781, with its gambrel roof, is a type used here and at Portsmouth during the latter part of the 18th century. This roof form, economical of materials as it is, does not seem to be very appropriate for the hot Virginia climate, and was not much used after 1800. It is now the property of the United States.

The base of the Yorktown monument was designed by Richard Morris Hunt and erected between 1881-84. It is an especially successful, though Victorian, piece of monumental architecture, and still makes its point in spite of the fact that the original figure on the top of the column was destroyed by lightning and replaced by the present one some years ago.

The National Park Service's Visitor Center at Yorktown will furnish information about open hours of those buildings on exhibition.

B 18   **Fort Monroe** *1819-34*   *Hampton, Fort Monroe (Old Point Comfort) 8-5*

Fort Monroe, built to protect the Hampton Roads area, is the largest enclosed fortification in this country, and was so successful that it never fell into the hands of an enemy. Its great masonry walls, though severely plain, gain interest through the convolutions of the shape of the fort itself, a shape forced by

B19

B20

64   Architecture in Virginia

the military demands of the structure. This masterpiece of military architecture was designed by General Simon Bernard, a man who had served as a military engineer under Napoleon. He migrated to this country in 1816; President Monroe made him a brevet brigadier general in the U. S. Army; and he was placed at the head of a Board of Engineers charged with constructing a system of coastal defenses. General Bernard returned in 1831 to France, where he twice rose to the post of Minister of War.

B 19 **Hampton Institute** *1868; 1874; 1882; 1886   Hampton (On Route 60 off Interstate 64) Open to visitors on the Hampton Tour*

Hampton Institute was founded in 1868 with only 15 students, who lived in makeshift quarters, the girls in a wooden building, the boys in tents. By 1874 Virginia Hall, designed by Richard Morris Hunt, was being built to contain "a chapel, with seating for four hundred people, an industrial room for the manufacture of clothing, and for instruction in sewing in all its branches; a dining room able to accommodate two hundred and seventy-five boarders; a large laundry and kitchen, besides quarters for twelve teachers and sleeping rooms for one hundred and twenty girls." The work on the building was largely done by the students under the supervision of Albert Howe as superintendent and Charles D. Cake as foreman.

Hunt also had designed an Academic Hall, which burned c. 1880. In a surviving letter from the president of the Institute to Hunt, he was asked to design a new Academic Hall (finished 1882) and to "use the old foundations. Effect of buttresses on old building not good. Make building strong and plain—no attempt at ornament." The difference between Hunt's Virginia Hall, a typical, well articulated Victorian building, and his second Academic Hall, which, though "strong and plain" is also full of interest and variety through its use of brick of two colors, marks his advance as a designer and his ability to solve specific problems in a personal way.

The third notable building at Hampton Institute is the Memorial Church, designed by J. C. Cady in 1886. The tower, 150 feet high, of this Romanesque Revival church gives great emphasis to the square nave. The brick has been carried through to make the interior finish of the walls, and the building itself has been almost untouched since it was finished. Even the pews built by the students to seat a congregation of a thousand are still in place. The Victorian sense of style is well demonstrated in the design of this nondenominational chapel.

B 20 **Tazewell Hall** *first half of the 18th century; mid-19th century; c. 1900; 1965   Newport News (1109 Riverside Dr.)*

Tazewell Hall has a restless history. Built first, at an unidentified date, for Sir John Randolph, it was moved c. 1900 from the end of Elizabeth Street in Williamsburg to a site facing the street. Before that it had suffered from a good bit of 19th century work, including a staircase at the end of the entrance salon. Finally the house was demolished. The magnificent

B21

B22

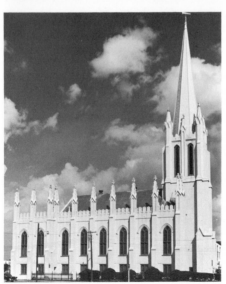

B23

66   Architecture in Virginia

paneling was saved, however, and eventually fell into the hands of the present owners, Mr. and Mrs. Lewis A. McMurran, Jr., who have recently built a new Tazewell Hall to house this splendid 18th century woodwork. They have stripped away the 19th century additions, restoring the mantels to early forms, and have chosen to use a full two stories for the entrance salon, a device allowing the restoration of a full entablature over the beautiful pilasters. The paneling in the house, especially in the drawing room and dining room, may be related to the 18th century handbook *Palladio Londinensis*, and, together with that at Carter's Grove, is certainly some of the most interesting in the State.

B 21 **Civic Center-City Hall Complex** *1964-65* *Norfolk* (*333 W. Freemason St.*) *Office hours*

Norfolk, having embarked on a vast renewal project, as have so many cities lately, has built, as a symbol of her energy and her confidence in her future, this expressive and *humane* civic complex. Her Courts Building, her City Hall, her Public Service Building and her Public Safety Building have been grouped by the architects, Vincent Kling and his associates Oliver and Smith, about a series of varied but unified open spaces that retain their civic scale without having lost their relationship to people. Great care has been taken with both detail and mass in these imaginative buildings. The City Hall has been given one of the six 1967 Honor Awards of the mid-Atlantic Region of the American Institute of Architects.

B 22 **Customs House** *1852* *Norfolk* (*W. Main St.*) *Weekdays 9-5*

Ammi B. Young, first supervising architect of the United States Treasury, designed both the Norfolk and the Charleston, S. C., customs houses. The Norfolk building boasts interior columns of cast iron and is an excellent example of the adaptation of a new material to a traditional form.

A black-and-white marble floor, part of which has been replaced, distinguishes the interior. The building is a notable essay in the late Classical Revival style, which continued to be a powerful influence until the Civil War. Twentieth century caution has filled in the original piercings of the iron risers of the handsome stairs.

B 23 **Freemason Street Baptist Church** *1849-50; 1895; 1897; 1915; 1950* *Norfolk* (*Bank & Freemason Sts.*) *Open during services*

Commissioned from Thomas U. Walter almost as soon as the congregation was formed in 1848, this large and strong Gothic Revival church was described in an early history of Norfolk as being "one of the handsomest and unquestionably the most ornamental building in the city. It is indeed, a noble temple of worship, and splendid monument of human art." It is remarkable in another way, for the boldness of its design matches the boldness of its congregation, which had only thirteen heads of families when it was begun. An 1895 addition at the rear and two additions of 1915 and 1958 have enlarged it from its former

B24

B25

B26

68   Architecture in Virginia

and quite wonderful proportions. Its steeple, topped with a trumpet 200 feet above the sidewalk, blew over in 1879 and was replaced by a steel one in 1897.

B24 **General Douglas MacArthur Memorial** *1847-50; 1960-61   Norfolk (City Hall Ave. & Bank St.) Weekdays 10-5; Sun. 11-6*

Designed by William R. Singleton, with Thomas U. Walter consulting and designing the dome, this building was put up as Norfolk's courthouse between 1847 and 1850. Its broad sweep of steps up to its impressive portico with its gigantic two-story Tuscan columns, its pilastered walls and the columned drum of its dome make it one of Virginia's best remaining Classical Revival buildings. In 1960-61 its interior was transformed into the General Douglas MacArthur Memorial by William and Geoffory Platt, with Finley Ferguson associated. The vigor of the exterior was retained during this transformation, and, interestingly, it expresses, though in different form, the same confidence to be sensed in the new Civic Center.

B25 **Hermitage Foundation** *1906-46   Norfolk (North Shore Road west of Hampton Blvd.) April 1-Labor Day, 1-5; Winter, 12-5   Fee*

Mrs. William Sloane, for whom the Hermitage was erected, carried on almost continuous building operations and changes over a long period. Attribution to a single architect is difficult, but the west end of the house is credited to Wickham Taylor. A joiner and woodcarver, Charles J. Woodson, worked there for many years, while French and Co. of New York and Watson of Philadelphia worked on some of the interiors. Thus, this romantic Tudor house was built in a manner similar to its prototypes, and, even while serving its new purpose as a museum for its present owner, the Hermitage Foundation, has recaptured much of the atmosphere of that very non-classic period.

B26 **Moses Myers House** *1791-92; 1797   Norfolk (Bank & Freemason Sts.) April 1-Labor Day, weekdays, 10-5; Sun., 11-6; Winter, weekdays, 12-5; Sun., 1-5   Fee*

One of the few surviving examples of the late 18th century town house in Tidewater Virginia, the Moses Myers house has remained remarkably intact because the original family continued to occupy it until the 1930's. An addition at the back consisting of a dining room and a kitchen connected by porches to the main house has been attributed to Benjamin Henry Latrobe. The simplicity of the late Georgian exterior does not prepare one for either the very large entrance hall, parallel to the principal front, or the interior's elaborate Federal scheme of plaster decoration, which may well have been added at the time of the addition of the carefully and handsomely designed dining room. Although the molds for this plaster work are in the Metropolitan Museum in New York, the name of the artisan is unknown, as is the name of the original architect. The City of Norfolk, which now owns the house, is fortunate in the survival of much of the original furniture, which has been used in the exemplary restoration of the house.

B27

B28

B29

B30

B 27 **Old Norfolk Academy Building** *1840   Norfolk   (420   Bank   St.)*
Mon.-Fri., 9-5

Thomas U. Walter, who also designed the Gothic Revival
Freemason Street Baptist Church, chose the Greek Revival for
this strong and masculine temple-form building, erected to
house the Norfolk Academy. As early as 1728 land had been set
aside for an Academy, which was first under the control of the
Borough authorities, but which was incorporated by the
General Assembly in 1804. The cornerstone of this building was
laid on May 25, 1840, and it was used by the Academy until
1940. It now belongs to the city of Norfolk and houses the
Juvenile and Domestic Relations Court.

B 28 **Robert M. Hughes Memorial Library, Old Dominion College**
1959   Norfolk (Hampton Blvd. at 48th St.) College hours

Designed by Edward Durrell Stone, with Oliver and Smith
associated, this library is completely encased in a solar block
screen, behind which are walls of glass. This device allows
a very open feeling in all exterior rooms without glare or heat.
The solar screen, indeed, has proved its utilitarian effectiveness by reducing both the heating and the cooling loads for the
building. But it has also given the building a beautiful unity
and a repose not always found in libraries today.

B 29 **St. Paul's Church** *1739; 1786; 1901; 1913   Norfolk (Church St. &*
City Hall Ave.) Weekdays, 9-4:30; Sun., 2-4:30

This Latin-cross plan church has had a difficult history of
survival. Burned in 1776, it was rebuilt in 1786, suffered
various vicissitudes during the early 19th century, was occupied
by troops from 1863 to 1865, had its present separate belfry
built in 1901, its cupola somewhat later, and its interior restored in 1913. What is original, then, is the brickwork, together with its window openings. In the south gable may still
be seen a brick marked "1739 SB," the initials standing for
Col. Samuel Boush, who is believed to have given the land,
the bricks and the nails for the building. The church has an
exceptionally beautiful churchyard, whose wall was built in
1759, which helps this handsome building retain its early aspect in spite of its many rebuildings.

B 30 **Virginia National Bank** *1966-67   Norfolk   (1   Commercial   Pl.)*
Banking hours

This great skyscraper is another of the buildings to take its
place in the renaissance of Norfolk. It has been given a three-
acre site where Norfolk began over three centuries ago, and is
surrounded by a well-landscaped podium. The architects,
Skidmore, Owings and Merrill with Williams and Tazewell
and Associates, have triumphed over the usual design limita-
tion of the skyscraper—the repetitive story—by quickening the
rhythm of the building by its bold projections. This new
building should become one of the symbols of the vigorous
commercial life of this maritime city.

B31

B32

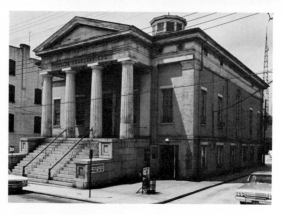

B33

B34

B31 **Battersea** *c. 1760; early 19th century; c. 1910* Petersburg *(Battersea Lane, off Washington St.) Private*

Built for Col. John Bannister on his return from an English education, Battersea was described in 1781 by the Marquis de Chastellux as "Mr. Bannister's handsome country-house . . . It is decorated rather in the Italian, than the English or American style, having three porticos at the three principal entries . . ." The Palladian, five-part plan of the house was the basis for the "Italian" description, but that impression has been strengthened by the early 19th century coating of stucco and the insertion of the triple and Palladian windows. At some time, what was probably a two-story portico was reduced to the present one-story porch, and, c. 1910, a small addition was added to the east. The great feature of the interior is the beautiful stairway with its Chinese Chippendale rail. The house is now owned by Mr. and Mrs. Russell S. Perkinson.

B32 **City Market** *1878-79* Petersburg *(Block surrounded by Old St., Cockade Alley, River St. & Rock St.) By arrangement, caretaker*

The fourth market building to have been put up on the site, this octagonal building is 93 feet in diameter. Its corbeled brick at the cornice line, its central, wooden cupola and the elaborate iron brackets that help support the exterior canopy give it a distinction not always present in such utilitarian structures. It is owned by the City of Petersburg.

B33 **Exchange Building** *1839-40* Petersburg *(East Bank St.) Open when Court is not in session*

Built by a group of businessmen to display tobacco and cotton and to hold auctions and sales, the Exchange Building was designed by a Mr. Berrien of New York. It later became the Bank of the City of Petersburg and now houses the Domestic Relations and Police Court Departments of Petersburg. Mr. Berrien gave the building the dignity of the Greek Revival, the liveliness of a dome and cupola and some interesting window detail in the frieze. The building has also had the distinction of appearing on some banknotes issued by the Bank of the City of Petersburg in 1862.

B34 **Farmer's Bank of Virginia** *1817; c. 1870 (?)* Petersburg *(Bollingbrook St. & Cockade City Alley)*

One of the state's oldest extant banking buildings, this beautiful Federal structure was recently restored. The delicate woodwork of the cashier's living quarters on the upper floors is almost intact, and it was no great task to free the ground floor entrance and banking room from its Victorianized façade. The bank, prosperous enough to have eight branches, did not survive the Civil War. The building was then put to other uses until 1963, when it was purchased by the Association for the Preservation of Virginia Antiquities, which is directing its restoration, a project to include the guardhouse, the smoke house and the kitchen at the rear, as well as the banking building itself.

B35

B36

B37

B38

B35 **Tabb Street Presbyterian Church** *1844* *Petersburg* *(W. Tabb St.) Inquire at Church House*

One of the architectural mysteries of Virginia is the unknown designer of this Greek Revival church. The handling of the Doric portico, of the body of the church and of the Corinthian order in the interior denotes the control of a very certain architectural hand. Yet no name has been associated with this outstanding building, which all too obviously was *not* put together either carelessly or cheaply. It is a knowing and fine example of the Greek Revival.

B36 **Trapezium House** *1815* *Petersburg* *(N. Market St.)*

Built without right angles in order "to keep spirits away," this charming little Federal house both gains and loses from the eccentric whims of its original owner, Charles O'Hara. It gains the charm of irregularity—even its stairs are at odd angles to the walls—but it loses a little in the very peculiar perspectives one sees from the exterior. Only the firm regularity of the Federal placement of openings and the simplicity of detail save it from too dashing an effect. It is now owned by the Association for the Preservation of Petersburg Antiquities.

B37 **Old Norfolk Naval Hospital** *1827-32; 1907; 1942-43* *Portsmouth (From Norfolk-Portsmouth tunnel, right on Washington St., left on Crawford St.) Grounds only*

The original building of this hospital was a hollow square, 172 feet by 192 feet, "embellished," as its architect John Haviland said, "with a bold Doric Portico of ten columns accessible by twenty steps that stretch ninety-two feet the whole length of the portico." Unfortunately this first building was gutted in 1907, when the present dome was added and extensions were built. Further additions were made in 1942-43. Fortunately the "bold Doric Portico" survives, though the sweep of steps has been shortened by the pylons at either end.

The original hospital, the first to be built from the Hospital Fund, was remarkably up to date, with its fireproof construction, its water closets and its balconies onto which every room opened. Its scheme was apparently so grand that its trustees, worried about the expense, sent Charles Bulfinch to make a report on it. He stated that the "location of the hospital appears well calculated for health and to gratify the feelings of hardy seamen for whom it is raised; that the work is well executed and does credit to the science and skill of the architect, John Haviland, Esq. and to the diligence and attention of Mr. William Wells who has superintended the execution of the work." This fragment of a noble building corroborates Bulfinch's opinion.

B38 **Old Town** *late 18th and early 19th centuries* *Portsmouth (Excellent walking tour map free from Chamber of Commerce)*

Established in 1752 by Col. William Crawford, who projected a fine city plan, of which a portion may still be seen (at the courthouse and church corners—they were to have been bal-

B39

B40

B41

76 Architecture in Virginia

anced by a jail and market), Portsmouth developed a vigorous and characteristic architecture, much of which has survived. An area lying between the Navy Shipyard Museum and the Naval Hospital has been designated as the "Old Town." The gambrel roofs of the late 18th century houses contrast with the high English basements of many of the early 19th century houses. Not only may one find a business block of c. 1840 in this area, but the visitor should also examine the later buildings both for their design interest and for their continuing and imaginative use of iron, which had also been well used on the earlier and more traditional structures. This area is also fortunate in having retained its granite curbs and brick or stone slab sidewalks. It is, in fact, one of the "undiscovered" but very rich Virginia architectural compounds.

B39 **Portsmouth Public Library** *1908-09; 1931-32; 1964 Portsmouth (601 Court St.) Library hours*

First designed as a post office by James Knox Taylor in 1908-09, and enlarged in 1931-32, this eclectic building has recently been remodeled into a most successful city library by the office of Glenn Yates, Jr., and James D. Boggs. Little was done to the exterior of the handsome building other than replacing window sash and the railing, sandblasting, cleaning and re-landscaping. The interior, on the other hand, was transformed into a contemporary library, and its demonstration of the compatibility of old and new won for it awards for excellence from the Virginia Chapter of the American Institute of Architects in 1964 and nationally from the American Library Association.

B40 **Warehouse Building No. 17** *1835 Portsmouth (Navy Yard) By application*

The Navy Yard at Portsmouth has retained a group of its early shop and warehouse buildings. They are well worth examination, not only as examples of warehouse architecture but also as expressions of building for a function and purpose. Building No. 17, for example, gains interest from its well marked rhythm, its strong but subtle brick cornice and its large but properly scaled windows. The Navy Yard, indeed, is full of unusual forms peculiar to its needs (dry docks, for instance), and should be looked at with some care.

B41 **Adam Thoroughgood House** *c. 1636-40; 1742-45; 1957 Virginia Beach (From Norfolk, Route 166 to Route 13, right on Pleasure House Road, follow signs; or Route 60 northeast of Norfolk, right on Pleasure House Road, follow signs) Weekdays 10-5; Sun. 11-6 Fee*

One of the oldest houses extant in Virginia, this little building was put up by Adam Thoroughgood on land granted him in 1636. A stairway, instead of the original ladder, was installed in 1742, and three years later the ceilings were plastered, the fireplaces made smaller, and wainscoting and other paneling installed. When the City of Norfolk acquired the house in 1957, its 18th century dormers were removed and the diamond-paned windows were restored to the first floor, though the stairway

B42

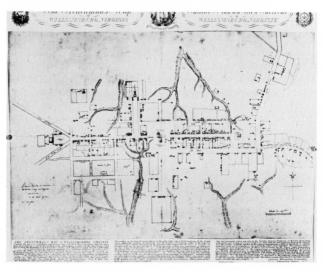

and the paneling were left in the interior. Thus the house re-acquired its 17th century exterior aspect with its small mullioned windows, vast chimneys and unbroken roof.

B42 **Old Cape Henry Lighthouse** *1791*   *Virginia Beach, Fort Story*   *9-6*

The federal government built its first lighthouse here at Cape Henry. It was first lighted in October, 1792, and served almost a century. Octagonal rather than round, built of cut stone, it is still sturdy, and its great lantern has very large glass areas for the transmission of light. This first United States example of a necessary but not very frequent building type has been designated a Registered National Historic Landmark, and is administered by the Association for the Preservation of Virginia Antiquities.

Williamsburg

Williamsburg, as Middle Plantation, was in existence as early as 1633, but it remained a tiny, stockaded settlement throughout the 17th century. As late as 1699 it was described by a hopeful student as having "great helps and advances towards the beginning of a Town, a Church, an ordinary, several stores, two Mills, a smiths shop, a Grammar School, and above all the Colledge."

After the statehouse at Jamestown burned in 1698, the seat of the Colony's government was moved (in 1699) to Middle Plantation, when it was renamed Williamsburg. Just six years later Robert Beverley said the then governor (Nicholson) "flatter'd himself with the fond Imagination, of being the Founder of a new City. He mark's out the Streets in many Places, so as that they might represent the Figure of a W, in Memory of his late Majesty King William . . . There he provid'd a stately Fabrick to be erected, which he placed opposite to the College, and graced it with the magnificent Name of the Capitol." Only a few years later, however, we are told that Governor Spotswood altered "the Streets of the Town . . . from the fanciful Forms of Ws. and Ms. to much more Conveniences."

By 1722 Hugh Jones wrote that the "buildings here . . . are justly reputed the best in all the English America, and are exceeded by few of their kind in England . . . The town is laid out regularly in lots or square portions, sufficient each for a house and garden; so that they don't build contiguous, whereby may be prevented the spreading danger of fire; and this also affords a free passage for the air, which is very grateful in violent hot weather."

It was Governor Spotswood who helped so much to transform the village into a proper governmental center during the early 18th century. Sir William Keith said that Spotswood "was well acquainted with Figures, and so good a Mathematician, that his Skill in Architecture, and in the laying out of Ground to the Best Advantage is yet to be seen in Virginia, by the Building of an elegant safe Magazine, in the Centre of Williamsburgh, and in the considerable Improvements which he made to the Governor's House and Gardens," This governor

LEGEND
1. INFORMATION
2. CAFETERIA
3. ADMINISTRATION
4. MOTOR HOUSES

NEW INFORMATION CENTER AREA
WILLIAMSBURG, VIRGINIA
COLONIAL WILLIAMSBURG, INC.
ARCHITECT'S OFFICE

also worked on the College, Bruton Parish Church, for which he supplied the first "draught," and, as we have just seen, Williamsburg's city plan.

Williamsburg prospered from the many people who came to it for the meetings of the Assembly and the many and various sorts of courts that sat there, and because of this prosperity there seemed no need for industry. The city was also a lively place, with balls, gambling, concerts, a theater and races held "twice a year; that is, every spring and fall, or autumn. Adjoining to the town is a very excellent course, for either two, three or four mile heats."

In 1780 the capital was moved to Richmond, and Williamsburg, so careless about industry, had no choice but to wither. The decay was not immediate, for a member of the French forces pointed out in 1781 that "upon nearly all the houses are lightning rods. The chimneys are all of brick, often outside the houses and rising far above the roofs. Almost all of them are capped with cut stones placed carefully and symetrically. Also upon the roofs are to be seen fire ladders," but by 1782 the picture was radically changed.

The Rev. Francis Asbury preached in the courthouse on December 11, 1782, and noted that "the place has suffered and is suffering; the palace, the barracks, and some good dwelling-houses burnt. The capitol is no great building, and is going to ruin; the exterior of the college is not splendid, and but few students; the Bedlam-house is desolate, but whether because none are insane, or all are equally mad, it might, perhaps, be difficult to tell."

These observations are confirmed by many other writers, especially Jedidiah Morse, who in 1787 said that "everything in Williamsburgh appears dull, forsaken and melancholy—no trade—no amusements, but the infamous one of gaming —no industry, and very little appearance of religion. The unprosperous state of the college, but principally the removal of the seat of government, have contributed much to the decline of this city."

In 1816 it was stated that "if it wasn't for the College, and the Court, and the Lunatics . . . what would become of it [Williamsburg]. As it is, it is but the shadow of itself, and even that seems passing away." And in 1824 another visitor saw that "some of the houses are fallen down; and the whole village bears the marks of poverty."

But by 1855 an anonymous letter struck a much more optimistic note by pointing out that the "City of Williamsburg is prospering. Improvements of all kinds are giving the ancient metropolis an air of youth which emphatically predicts its future prominence among the cities of the Old Dominion."

Nevertheless nearly three quarters of a century were still to pass before this Sleeping Beauty of American cities was to awaken from her long sleep, thanks to the generosity of the Rockefeller family. Her handsome city plan intact, many of her original buildings occupied, she has become since 1926 not only an example of restoration and reconstruction on a munificent scale, but a pioneering laboratory in the methods of restoration.

Although almost every building in the restored area of the

B43

B44

B45

B46

*city is worthy of attention, the following buildings are especially
noteworthy. The open hours of the exhibition buildings and the
very useful* Official Guidebook and Map *may be obtained
at the Information Center.*

B43 **Armistead House** *1858   Duke of Gloucester St.*

This Greek Revival building, one of the very few to have been
built in Williamsburg, was described in the *Williamsburg
Weekly Gazette* for June 30, 1858, as a "Handsome Building—
Lemeul J. Bowden building a fine residence Purchased lot 53 x
40 from Episcopal Church. Built of Baltimore stock brick—
with granite silles and iron caps to the doors and windows.
House contains 3 stories, including a spacious basement—4
room and two halls or entries on each floor; hall 10 ft. wide and
without obstruction, the stairways being run up through side
entries 8 feet wide; doors and windows are very large, some of
them 7 to 10 ft. wide. House surmounted by an elegant hip roof.
Contractor: Henry M. Bowden
Masons: Messrs. Taylor & Womack of Richmond & E. W.
Teagle of Gloucester."
Judge Robert T. Armistead, its present owner, is the third
Judge Armistead to have occupied this house, unusual as to
both style and date in the Williamsburg milieu.

B44 **Blair House** *18th century   Duke of Gloucester St.*

Built first at an uncertain date in the early 18th century, this
house, named for a late owner, John Blair, Jr., had a two-room,
central-hall and lean-to-at-the-rear plan. Later in the century a
large room and lean-to were added to the west, thus making the
west chimney an interior rather than an exterior one as it had
been originally. This later addition carefully preserved the detail of the earlier portion of the house with its transomed door
and its hipped roof dormer. Accounts for 1789-91 for the brick-
layer and plasterer, Humphrey Harwood, list a marble mantel,
which is still in place. The house is now owned by Colonial
Williamsburg.

B45 **Brush-Everard House** *1717-19; wings later, date unknown   Palace
Green*

Built for John Brush, this early home is an excellent example
of the small, frame house that was popular in Williamsburg.
A late owner, Thomas Everard, may have built the two wings
that turn its plan into a U. The notable feature of the house is
its staircase, which is more expansive and elaborate than
one would expect in a house of this size, as it has step brackets
carved in a manner very like those at Carter's Grove and
Tuckahoe. The house is now owned by Colonial Williamsburg.

B46 **Bruton Parish Church** *1715; 1750-52; 1769   Duke of Gloucester St.*

Replacing an earlier church, the present Bruton Parish Church
was designed by Governor Spotswood, and first completed in
1715; its chancel was lengthened in 1750-52; and its present

B47

B48

tower was built in 1769. It is the oldest surviving cruciform church in Virginia. As it was the official church of the Colony, it was paid for in part by the General Assembly, who occupied the transepts when in session in Williamsburg. The churchyard wall dates from 1754. The steep roof gives the building a slight Gothic air in spite of the semi-circular headed windows and doors and the cornice based on classical precedent. This transitional air, perhaps derived from the earlier and more frankly Gothic (?) building, is somewhat confusing.

Hugh Jones called it "a large strong piece of brickwork in the form of a cross, nicely regular and convenient, and adorned as the best churches in London," in 1722, soon after it was finished. This is still a good description of the building, whose exterior is largely original, but whose interior, due to many 19th century changes and a major restoration of 1905, is largely a careful reconstruction of 1938. The church is still owned by Bruton Parish and it is still noted for its music, just as it was when it brought its first organ from England in 1752 and its first organist, Peter Pelham (the stepbrother of John Singleton Copley), down from Boston.

B47 Capitol *1701-04; 1747-53* *Capitol Square*

First erected under the supervision of Henry Cary, the master builder, this structure burned in 1747. It was built again, with less distinction, between 1747 and 1753, and burned a second time in 1832. The present building, owned by Colonial Williamsburg, is a reconstruction of the *first* Capitol and rests largely on the original foundations.

This 1701-04 Capitol was described c. 1722 as being "in the form of an H nearly; the General Court taking up one side below stairs; the middle being an handsome portico leading to the clerk of the Assembly's office, and the House of Burgesses on the other side; which last is not unlike the House of Commons.

"In each wing is a good stair case, one leading to the council chamber, where the governor and Council sit in very great state, in imitation of the King and Council, or the Lord Chancellor and House of Lords.

". . . upon the middle is raised a lofty cupola with a large clock."

One of the most successful of the reconstructions in Williamsburg, this handsome, sturdy building is now used once every other session of the Virginia Legislature for the same purpose as its original predecessor.

B48 Courthouse *1770; 1911* *Duke of Gloucester St.*

This courthouse, replacing an earlier one, presents an architectural (or perhaps economic) puzzle, for its portico was without its columns until the renovation of 1911, when ill-fitting and badly shaped ones were provided. During its restoration in 1932 by Colonial Williamsburg, which now owns it, it was decided to remove the 1911 columns and not to replace them. The reason for their original omission has not been discovered. The T-shape of the building follows the earlier pattern of Virginia courthouses.

B49

B49

B50

John Ferdinand Dalziel Smyth noted c. 1770 that "Williamsburg is also the county-town of James-city county [as well as being the Colonial capital]; where the courts of common pleas are held monthly as they are also in every county in the colony . . . The quarter sessions are also held quarterly in each county . . ." Thus we know that the courthouse was quite busy with legal affairs. Placed on one side of Market Square, it must have dominated the livelier and more parochial aspects of Williamsburg's official life.

B49 **Governor's Palace** *c. 1706-20; 1751* *Palace Green*

Soon after the removal of the seat of government to Williamsburg, the Palace was described as "a House for the Governor, not the largest, but by far the most beautiful of all the other [public buildings]. It was granted by the Assembly in Governor *Nott's* time, begun in President *Jenings* his time, but received its Beauty and Conveniency, from the many Alterations and Decorations, of the present Governor Colonel *Spotswood:* Who, to the lasting Honour and Hapiness of the Country, arrived there, while this House was carrying up." Unfortunately, the "lasting Honour and Hapiness" had disappeared before the end of the century, for Thomas Jefferson wrote in 1781, "The Palace is not handsome without: but it is spacious and commodious within, is prettily situated, and, with the grounds annexed to it, is capable of being made an elegant seat." Jefferson's scheme for making it an "elegant seat" was to transform it into a porticoed, temple form building, and his drawings for this idea survive.

The Palace, being used as a hospital during the Revolution, was burned in 1781 through the carelessness of the patients. In 1930-32, a high school that had been built on the site was demolished, the original foundations laid bare, and the present noble reconstruction was erected. It seems clear from this building that the original Palace, with its 1706-20 central portion, its 1751 ballroom-supper-room wing, its detached dependencies and its extensive gardens, which have been successfully re-established, was the most elaborate domestic complex in the Colony. Colonial Williamsburg now owns the Palace.

B50 **Information Center** *1956-57*

At the edge of the restored area, Colonial Williamsburg has built a most successful information center, motor house and cafeteria. Designed by the architectural staff of Colonial Williamsburg with Harrison and Abramowitz as consultants, it is thoroughly contemporary, but does not destroy the totality of the effect made by 18th century Williamsburg. The Information Center, itself, is given form by the two theatres contained within the building. The Motor House, aside from the care exercised on all its details, makes its point of expansive hospitality primarily through its site plan. Placed in a large pine grove, it has enough land not only to prevent crowding but to allow for a marked measure of privacy for both man and car, thus continuing the best traditions of Virginia's innkeepers throughout four centuries.

B51

B52

B53

B54

88   Architecture in Virginia

B51 **Ludwell-Paradise House** *c. 1737*   *Duke of Gloucester St.*

The first house to be acquired for restoration in Williamsburg, this early-Georgian residence needed little repair to bring it back to its original appearance. It was built by Philip Ludwell II as a town house, and its handsome use of brick marks it as one of the more luxurious houses of the time, in spite of its apparent simplicity. Its effect depends almost entirely on the subtlety of its proportions. It is now owned by Colonial Williamsburg.

B52 **Peyton Randolph House** *c. 1715; c. 1750*   *Nicholson St.*

This large residence has a most unusual history. It began as two houses, that on the west having been started by William Robertson in 1715 or 1716, and that at the east end, sometime before 1724. A little later the same person became the owner of these two houses and, c. 1750, built the center section. Today the west wing and the center section are original, while the east wing, which had previously been demolished, is a reconstruction. The west wing, with its central chimney, corner fireplaces and two-story "porch" tower on the north, reminiscent of the 17th century houses, is especially notable not only for its plan, which is atypical for Williamsburg, but for its paneling on both floors, which is the best original paneling extant in Williamsburg. This interesting and unusual house is now owned by Colonial Williamsburg.

B53 **Public Records Office** *1748*   *Duke of Gloucester St.*

Frightened by the 1747 fire in the Capitol, the legislators had this semi-fireproof building put up for "the Preservation of the Public Records and Papers." Its floor was masonry, its window jambs and interior partitions brick, and its chimney caps were sloped to prevent downdrafts. Even the handsome door enframement was worked out in molded brick. This beautiful, mid-Georgian example of official architecture is a splendid illustration of the retention of human scale in a composition expressing the dignity of the state. It is now owned by Colonial Williamsburg.

B54 **Powder Magazine** *1715*   *Market Square*

This "elegant safe Magazine" is one of the few surviving pieces of colonial military architecture in the State. Built under Governor Spotswood, it was described in 1722 by Hugh Jones as "a large octagon tower, which is the magazine or repository of arms and ammunition, standing far from any house except James Town Court-House." But a century later Charles Campbell called it "a small round brick edifice with a conical roof, and now converted into a Baptist meeting-house." It was *always* octagonal, and is largely original. It is still a center of military exercises and celebrations on official and holiday occasions. Although restored by Colonial Williamsburg and serving as one of its exhibition buildings, it is owned by the Association for the Preservation of Virginia Antiquities.

B55

B56

B57

B58

B55 **Semple House** *c. 1780*   *Francis St.*

Built at the very end of the period of Williamsburg's prosperity, the Federal exterior of the Semple house is largely unchanged, and its classicism is in strong contrast to the earlier Georgian buildings of the city. Recent research has strengthened the earlier attribution of the design to Thomas Jefferson, although this attribution is not yet certain. Named for Judge James Semple, an early (but not the first) owner, it is now owned by Colonial Williamsburg.

B56 **St. George Tucker House** *c. 1714; 1788-95*   *Nicholson St.*

Built for William Levingston as a story-and-a-half house facing Palace Green, the original building was moved to face Nicholson Street in 1788. Between then and 1795, St. George Tucker changed it to a two story-structure and added the present wings. The great exterior chimneys and the irregular but harmonious massing of the house are the major elements of its charm, while they demonstrate the possibility of achieving compatibility between building operations of widely differing dates.

B57 **Wetherburn's Tavern** *c. 1740 (with later additions) Duke of Gloucester St.*

Built first as a residence, this building was better known as a tavern, and its best known proprietor was Henry Wetherburn. It has been found that there were at least ten stages of development in this building, which has just been restored to its condition of c. 1760-80. It is one of the few early taverns to have survived and, as such, is a valuable document of this traditional Virginia type. It is presently owned by the estate of Mrs. Virginia B. Haughwout, and the restoration is being carried out by Colonial Williamsburg.

B58 **Wren Building, College of William and Mary** *1695-99;   1705; 1729-32; 1859; 1862   College Yard*

One of the earliest public, or academic, buildings to survive in this country, the Wren building has passed through many vicissitudes. All three fires (1705, 1859 and 1862) did extensive damage, and after the last it was rebuilt as a Victorian "Old Main Hall." The walls, however, are largely original, and although the chapel was not built until 1729-32, the building has been restored to the 1715 period.

Hugh Jones said, in 1722, that it was "a lofty pile of brick . . . adorned with a cupola. At the north end runs a large wing, which is a handsome hall, answerable to which the chapel is to be built; and there is a spacious piazza on the west side, from one wing to the other . . . The building is beautiful and commodius, being first modelled by Sir Christopher Wren, adapted to the nature of the country by the gentlemen there; and since it was burnt down, it has been rebuilt, and nicely contrived, altered and adorned by the ingenious direction of Governor Spotswood . . ."

In 1731-32 it was called "an handsome Pyle of Brick" but

B58

B59

fifty years later Jefferson, though using the word "pile" used it in another connotation when he called the Wren building and the hospital "rude, mis-shapen piles, which, but that they have roofs, would be taken for brick-kilns."

Before 1777 an addition to the west was planned to create a courtyard and a second building of the size of the first. It was noticed by a 1777 visitor that "there is also the Foundation of a new Building which was intended for an Addition to the College, but has been discontinued on Account of the present Troubles."

After the 1859 fire William Barton Rogers had talked with the Visitors and reported that "the old foundations and the front wall will be retained, but of course a more convenient interior has been planned."

One should note also the President's House (1732-33) and the Brafferton (1723), not quite identical buildings flanking the approach to the Wren Building. William Hugh Grove wrote in 1731-32 that "a separate building called Brotherton house" was used for "educating Indians in Christianity where they learn to read write & Gable their prayers twice a day & may be bound to trades but must return to the old way of life & carry more Vices away with them than they fellows ever know . . ."

These three buildings make up a most ordered and formalized group, and were far in advance of other academic establishments of the time architecturally. One would suspect, however, that the fires, the adaptation "by the gentlemen there," and the "ingenious direction of Governor Spotswood" had excised almost every trace of Wren from the central edifice. The College of William and Mary has never relinquished ownership of this beautiful group of buildings throughout its long history.

B 59 **Wythe House** *1752   Palace Green*

The most considerable private house in Williamsburg is this one built and probably designed by Col. Richard Taliaferro when he was repairing and adding the ballroom wing to the Palace. His daughter Elizabeth, at the time of her marriage to George Wythe, the jurist, probably brought him to live there. The house has the simplicity of dignity and an air of surety in its well-proportioned design that strengthens its attribution to Taliaferro's guiding genius. It is also notable for its outbuildings, which make of it an almost self-supporting enclave within the city. The house has survived without many changes, and the major task of the 1939-40 restoration, aside from the inevitable repairs and replacements, was the installation of appropriate mantels, as the originals have disappeared. The house is owned by Colonial Williamsburg.

Two major differences are apparent between this region and the preceding one. The first is that, because it was settled a little later than the more easily reached Tidewater area, its residents were not ready to build expansively until architecture in the Colony had moved into a more sophisticated stage. Consequently the plantation house, the most splendid of the pre-Revolutionary building types, is seen here at the very apex of its colonial development. The second difference is the presence of stone as a building material, used not only for entire buildings, as at Mt. Airy, but also for architectural emphasis, as at Aquia Church, a device that strengthens and monumentalizes architecture enormously.

Fredericksburg, the principal urban unit of the area, was for a long time a very lively port. It reflects this economic vigor in its considerable number of old buildings. One should walk about Fredericksburg with a good deal of attention, for, quite aside from its major architectural features, it is a city with many minor treasures.

Fredericksburg, November, 1862

C1

C2

C3

C₁ **Camden** *1857-59   Caroline Co. (2½ miles east on Route 17 from its intersection with Route 301 at Port Royal; left at sign on Route 686, straight ahead to end of road) Private*

A house of 1760-70, put up by John Pratt, some of whose walls may still be seen in t'e basement of Camden, was torn down to make way for the then-modernites of this splendid house, built for his bride by William Carter Pratt. The Baltimore architect N. G. Starkweather designed it, and his drawings are still preserved in the house. They show a tower that was shot away by a Yankee gunboat during the Civil War. Starkweather installed running water in every bedroom, gas lights and central heat. The original basins and parts of the heating system are still in use, and the house is now occupied by a Pratt descendant, Mr. Richard Turner Pratt.

In a letter of August 24, 1863, a guest described the house as "situated on a high bluff just over the river . . . The immediate grounds contain twenty acres, and are laid out with much taste, beautified with trees, shrubbery, arbors, and seats . . . One front of the house is towards the river, and from the yard to the river bank below is beautifully turfed, with a flight of steps running down to the boat landing, where was moored a row-boat, and where until the war was anchored a beautiful little yacht, which we found is now stored away in the barn . . . Each room is furnished and finished in a different kind of wood—oak, rosewood, mahogany, walnut, etc. The room I occupied was the rosewood. The mantles are all of white marble, and the locks and knobs of heavy silver plate."

Camden is one of the most complete and best preserved Victorian monuments in the Commonwealth.

C₂ **Blandfield** *c. 1750-70; 1844; 1859   Essex Co. (From Caret, ½ mile east on Route 17) Private*

Built for William Beverley, Blandfield has one of the most interesting plantation house plans in Virginia. The central space on the first floor is occupied not by a hall but by two large rooms with stair halls on either side. These lead up to a large cross hall on the second floor. The two connected, two-story dependencies are large enough to make this one of the most ample of the pre-Revolutionary domestic establishments in the colony. The exterior, with its low-pitched roof, its pedimented central pavilions and its fine cornice, has been little changed except for the porches, which replaced earlier ones (presumably two-story ones?) in 1859. Unfortunately, the interior was stripped by Van Ness in 1844, when he was in the area working at Mount Airy after its fire. Thus it is said that the Mount Airy fire was "the only fire that ruined two interiors." Blandfield is still in the hands of descendants, Mr. and Mrs. William N. Beverley.

C₃ **Brooke's Bank** *1731; c. 1946-47   Essex Co. (1 mile east of Loretto on Route 33, left on private road, left at fork to house) Private*

Brooke's Bank is most unusual in the history of Virginia architecture. Not only were its plans brought from England, which

C4

C5

C6

98   Architecture in Virginia

accounts for its design being some two or three decades in advance of its date, but it was built by a woman, Mrs. Sarah Talliafero Brooks, who emigrated with her children after she was widowed. This indomitable lady was well-served by her builders, who managed the rather more delicate proportions of the newer mid-Georgian era with skill, and who made the string course and the jack arches over the openings count as they should in so pure a design. The diamond-shaped patterns of glazed headers in the chimneys were, according to tradition, protection against witches, the one provincialism to be found. The superb paneling in the main rooms is still in place. Although the large wings on either side of the main house were added c. 1946-47, it is thought the small wings may possibly be original. The owners are Mr. and Mrs. Enos Richardson.

C4 **Elmwood** *c. 1775; 1852; 1965* *Essex Co.* (*Turn right on Route 640 from Route 17 1½ miles west of Loretto, for 100 yards; right on private road*) *Private*

Elmwood, with its eleven bays of openings, is one of the most prodigious of Virginia's pre-Revolutionary houses. Built for James Mercer Garnett, it was sadly altered in 1852; its entrance features were changed, some of its windows were lengthened, its original sash was removed, a stair tower was built, and its mantels were stripped away. Now its owner, Mr. Muscoe R. H. Garnett, is gradually bringing it back into some semblance of its former state. The Victorian stair tower has been removed, and it is possible once more to see the house in its original rectangular mass, characteristic of the years just before 1775. The paneling that survives, however, was inspired by earlier designs and is thoroughly mid-Georgian Baroque, a surprising anomaly in so late a house.

C5 **Vauter's Church** *c. 1719; 1731; 1827* *Essex Co.* (*Route 17, 15 miles north of Tappahannock*) *Scheduled services*

Vauter's Church was begun about 1719, with the south wing added, according to an inscribed brick, in 1731. It underwent some interior changes in 1827. It affords one of the best opportunities in the Commonwealth for the study of the beauties of colonial brickwork that has largely escaped the need for extensive repairs. The molded brick used at the doors forming a segmental pediment at one entrance and a triangular pediment at the other, the use of glazed headers over the field of the walls, and the line of glazed headers following the barge boards of the gables are all precisely and handsomely executed. Although the metal covering of the roof is not original, it is thought the cornice is, as are the two sets of entrance doors themselves. One sees more of colonial workmanship here than in almost any other Virginia parish.

C6 **Abingdon Parish Church** *1755; 1868* *Gloucester Co.* (*Route 17, 6 miles south of Gloucester*) *Scheduled services*

Abingdon Parish Church replaced an earlier (c. 1660) church, though whether the two were on the same spot or not is un-

C7

C8

known. The principal changes in the church occurred after the Civil War, during which the interior was wrecked. In 1868 new pews, new floors for the aisles, a new pulpit and a vesting room were installed. The exterior walls, however, are largely intact, as are the door enframements of molded brick, and the door and window frames with their keystones and pilaster capitals at the impost line. The doors themselves are probably not original, and, although the reredos is colonial, there is some doubt of its having been original with Abingdon. There is also some doubt that the continuation of the cornice horizontally across the gables is original, although it may have been. The Latin cross plan of Abingdon, the great width (35½′) of the nave and transepts, and the sophisticated architectural treatment of the door and window enframements all combine to make it an unusually spacious and knowledgeable example among the State's colonial churches.

C7 **Courthouse** *1766; 1894; 1956-57   Gloucester Co. (on Route 17) Mon.-Fri., 9-4; Sat., 9-12*

The Gloucester Courthouse was built to replace an earlier one. In 1894-95, the present portico was added, and some inside alterations were made. In 1956-57, the addition was built, and further interior changes were carried out. Thus we see a most interesting juxtaposition of the sympathetic, turn-of-the-century portico and window frames with the 18th century masonry and mass of the original. This courthouse is still used for its first purpose and is a focal point for the local government.

C8 **Rosewell** *1726   Gloucester Co. (From Yorktown, 8 miles north on Route 17, left on Route 614 for 2¾ miles, left on Route 632 for 2 miles, left on Route 644 to end of road; ruins are hidden in trees)*

Rosewell is both a romantic and a noble ruin, and stands as a monument to a dream never quite fulfilled. Begun in 1726 by Mann Page I, this largest of all the Colony's mansions was unfinished at his death in 1730. In 1744 his son, Mann Page II, had to petition the Assembly in order to sell some entailed land for funds to complete the house. It was sold by the Pages in 1838, at which time it was modernized by removing most of the paneling, and it burned in 1916. The daughter of Gov. Page described its great entrance hall and "grand staircase" as "an object of admiration to all who saw, or ascended it, and looked down upon the large hall, with its wainscoted walls of mahogany, and pilasters of Corinthian order, and the great hearth and marble mantelpiece." She continues, "All the rooms were wainscoted with wood of different colors, and had marble mantels, the ceilings were also of great height." Rosewell's three stories, as opposed to the usual two-storied Virginia house, its stone keystones and sills for the windows and its splendidly enriched stair made of it a unique mansion in the colony.

The last photographs of it before the fire, however, show it in such a depressed and neglected state, that one is almost grateful for the catastrophe that transformed it into this dream-like ruin.

C9

C10

C11

C12

C9 **Toddsbury** *c. 1658-60; c. 1690-1720; 1782; 1946   Gloucester Co.* *(From Gloucester, 3½ miles north on Route 14, right on Route 622 to private road) Private*

When Thomas Todd began this house it consisted of the hall and dining room and a Jacobean porch. Between 1690 and 1720 the parlor was added, the interiors were paneled, and the porch was enlarged by extending it to the end of the dining room. In 1782 it was enlarged again by being extended outward and by having a second floor added. At this time the two-story porch on the opposite side was added, its second story being enclosed later. The present kitchen was added in 1946.

Toddsbury, now owned by Mrs. Charles Beatty Moore, is fortunate in having had a series of owners who, when enlarging it, have been sympathetic with the very early gambrel-roofed design of the original, enhancing rather than destroying its impact.

C10 **Ware Parish Church** *1693-1715; 1854; 1902   Gloucester Co. (From Gloucester, 1 mile northeast on Routes 14 and 3) Scheduled services*

The notable features of Ware Parish Church are the variation and excellent preservation of its brick, its use of three doors in a rectangular church (almost the only example extant in the colony), the enormous thickness of its walls, and the unique, arched treatment of its principal entrance. Since it was "modernized" in 1854 and given a new slate roof and a plastered ceiling in 1902, its interior is largely "new." Its precise date is a little uncertain, some authorities preferring the earlier and some the later of those given for its first building.

C11 **Courthouse** *1735 Hanover Co. (17 miles north of Richmond on Route 301) Mon.-Fri., 9-4; Sat., 9-12*

This little T-shaped, early Georgian courthouse for Hanover County is similar to that in King William Co., built some ten years earlier. The beautiful brickwork of the Hanover Courthouse, its cornice and its steep roof are all related to the domestic work of the time, but its arcaded portico gives it the character of a public building without losing its human scale. Although it has been the scene of many historic associations and even survived a battle, its first lesson is that smallness and simplicity may be combined with dignity.

C12 **Scotchtown** *c. 1719   Hanover Co. (From Ashland, 7 miles northwest on Route 54, right on Route 685 for 1½ miles, left on Route 740 to marker) Apr. 1-Oct. 31 Wed. and Sat., 10-5; Sun., 2-5; otherwise by special appointment   Fee*

Charles Chiswell built this large (over 80 by 40 feet) house for what he hoped would be a Scottish community that would eventually be dominated by a castle! Although some of the castle's foundations were laid, an epidemic among the workmen stopped any further expansion. In 1824 the two chimneys of the house were replaced by four, but after the Association for the Preservation of Virginia Antiquities acquired Scotchtown in

C13

C14

C15

1953, these four were pulled down and the original two restored. These chimneys apparently make of the house one of the early examples of the use of the corner fireplace in the colony. Scotchtown has been, at various times, the home of both Patrick Henry and Dolly Madison, and its forthrightness, so strongly accentuated by its great, clipped gables, made of it a suitable residence for both.

C13 **Marmion** *c. 1725; c. 1770-80* *King George Co. (From Fredericksburg, 16 miles east on Route 3 to Comorn, left on Route 609 for 2 miles, right on private road at sign) By appointment*

There is much controversy over the dates for Marmion. Although some of the foundations may be 17th century, it would seem reasonable to suppose that the present house was largely erected c. 1725, and that the marbleizing of the paneling of the parlor, now in the Metropolitan Museum of Art in New York City, was carried out about 1770-80. The informality of the weather boarding, the clipped gables and asymmetry of the plan give the house a rural character.

Nevertheless Marmion, as it stands, is a most wonderful document. Except for the removal of the paneling of the parlor, the most sumptuous that had appeared in Virginia, the interior is unchanged. Some of the windows have lost their eighteenth century sash, but enough are left to give the right character to the house. And the outbuildings, placed at the four corners of a large square about the house, again demonstrate the interest in site planning held by the early Virginia builders. Marmion is now owned by Mr. Jay G. Powell.

C14 **Nanzatico** *c. 1775* *King George Co. (From Port Royal, north 2 miles on Route 301, right on Route 625 for 3¼ miles, right on 650 for 2 miles to river) Private*

Nanzatico is an excellent example of the formality it is possible to achieve in a timber building. It is also an excellent example of the increased architectonic quality demanded by the colonists just before the Revolution. Finally, it is also an excellent example of the increased knowledge of classical detail gained by the craftsmen of the time. All these characteristics are clearly seen in the exact symmetry in the exterior of the building, in the two-story pilasters, which, in effect, create a central pavilion without a projection of the building's mass, in the properly executed pediment with its delightful bull's eye window, and in the very adept way in which only the cornice of the beautiful entablature above the pilasters is carried around the entire house. Mr. Charles J. Davis is the present owner.

C15 **Powhatan** *c. 1825* *King George Co. (From Fredericksburg, 14 miles east on Route 3, right on Route 607 for 2 miles to private road) Private*

Powhatan, built by Edward Thornton Tayloe, is a most interesting adaptation of the 18th century five-part plan to 19th century neo-classicism. Even with the traditional materials of white-painted wood and red brick and the traditional massing of the house, the change in the proportions of the

C16

C17

C18

openings, the beautiful little Ionic portico and the change in detail give the house a very different aspect from its 18th century counterparts. The interiors are not original. The present owner is the Honorable Raymond Guest.

C16 **Courthouse** *1725   King William Co. (From West Point, 17 miles northwest on Route 30) Mon.-Fri., 9-4; Sat., 9-12*

Built only twenty-three years after the county was established on land partially donated by the county's first judge, this little T-shaped courthouse has been in continuous use since its completion. The central courtroom is plain and is flanked by a room for the judge on one side and a jury room on the other. This extremely functional plan is given architectural distinction by the building's cornice, its high, hipped roof and its arcade. The addition of the later buildings flanking the courthouse has enabled the county to retain the 1725 court virtually intact.

C17 **Elsing Green** *c. 1719 (?)   King William Co. (From Richmond, 20 miles north on Route 360, east at Manquin on Route 618 for 6½ miles, right on Route 629 1½ miles, left on Route 632 4 miles) Private*

Assigned a later date by one authority, Elsing Green's U-shaped plan and strong, plain court on the land side would make the earlier date given above possible. Whatever its date, the house is an unusually large and expansive one, with its wide cross hall, containing a staircase with a gentle ascent at each end, and its not quite centered entrance hall from the river side. The earlier house, which now acts as a dependency, increases this impression of size. Unfortunately, there was a disastrous fire in 1800, and much of the interior was destroyed at that time. The house was built for William Dandridge, and is now owned by Mr. and Mrs. Edgar Rivers Lafferty, Jr.

On May 9, 1849, John Toole wrote a lively description of Elsing Green. He was spending some time there executing a large group of family portraits, and said that it was "the largest private house I have ever seen. I sit now in the parlour, which seriously speaking, I am certain is as large as the body of the church in North Garden. The room in which I sleep is as large as the two lower rooms of our little house, and there are four of these rooms on a floor separated by passages about twenty feet wide. This old castle stands in the center of a field of 950 acres, on the Pamunkey River . . . Almost every day vessels of considerable size pass up or down the Pamunkey, for timber, corn, &c. and to me it is a pleasing sight to behold a fine broad sheet of water studded with white sails, and bordered by green forest trees."

C18 **Horn Quarter** *Early 19th century   King William Co. (Route 614, one mile south of 601) Private*

Horn Quarter was built for George Taylor on land that had come into his family through his mother. The house maintains the 18th century scheme of a central detached mass with chimneys on the outside walls, but executes this scheme in an up-to-

C19

C20

C21

108 Architecture in Virginia

date way, with Federal detail to be seen in its light window trim, fan-lighted doors and sunburst panels let into the walls between floors. It is now owned by Miss Doris Rowell.

C19 **Christ Church** *1732   Lancaster Co. (From Kilmarnock, 2½ miles southwest on Route 3, right on Route 222, first left turn on Route 646; church is straight ahead) Summer only*

This best preserved and most architectonic of Virginia's colonial churches probably owes both its preservation and its architectural character to having been built by Robert Carter. It was, in fact, only in 1960 that legal title to the church was acquired by the parish, so that for a very long period the building was not subject to changes needed for parish uses. Its donor and his family undoubtedly set its high architectural standard, too, a standard maintained until its completion even though Robert Carter had died some time before the church was finished.

The Latin cross plan, the plaster vaulted ceiling and the survival of the original pews, chancel furniture and pulpit make the interior as interesting as the exterior. The 35-inch-thick walls have served the church well, for only minor, though extensive, repairs have been necessary. The use of stone for the capitals and bases of the pilasters of the three doors and for the sills and keystones of the windows gives the building a refinement of detail that was unique in the colony. This refinement extends to the beautiful entablature with its cushion frieze. The north and south doors are original, as are the lunette of the west door and all the hardware. The slate roof replaced an earlier shingle roof in the early 1880's and was a gift of the Association for the Preservation of Virginia Antiquites. The present brick wall of the churchyard is a restoration on the foundations of the original wall.

This extraordinary building is one of the masterpieces of the early Georgian period surviving in the Commonwealth and, indeed, in the nation.

C20 **Boakahmar** *1964   Middlesex Co. (State Route 3) Private*

Built as a second home for the owners, Mr. and Mrs. Carlisle H. Humelsine, Boakahmar reflects their enthusiasm for yachting by its sweeping views of river, creek and cove. The hexagonal living room is given uninterrupted views by its shape, half of which projects beyond the backward sweeping wings containing bedrooms, kitchen and dining room. Though the form and intent of the house are contemporary, the architect, Eldridge T. Spencer, related it to the Virginia landscape with the warm wood tones of its cypress exterior and the pine and chestnut paneling of the interiors.

C21 **Tobacco Warehouse-Store** *c. 1763-67 (?) Urbana, Middlesex Co. (Virginia Ave., off Route 227 at town center) Open occasionally Contribution*

Great uncertainty exists over the date and the purpose of this early commercial building. Owned and restored by the Asso-

C22

C23

C24

ciation for the Preservation of Virginia Antiquities, it is given, by heavy shutters, plain gable roof, plank railing and sturdy exterior stairs, a crispness and a self-reliant character often lacking in today's small commercial structures.

C22 **Eyre Hall** *c. 1750; c. 1800; c. 1930   Northampton Co. (From Eastville south on Route 13 for 2½ miles, west on private road opposite Chesapeake turn-off for Route 636) Private*

Eyre Hall began as a small, two rooms-to-a-floor house with end chimneys, built for Little Eyre. About 1800 John Eyre built the gambrel-roofed addition, and soon after moved the 1750 portion enough to add two rooms between it and the 1800 addition. About 1930 the old kitchen was rebuilt on its foundations and joined to the house by a passageway. The gambrel roof of the 1800 portion seems to have been used in several parts of eastern Virginia about this time in spite of its heat-catching qualities in a hot climate. The principal feature of the interior is an exceptionally thick elliptical arch leading from the hall, an arch that contains, surprisingly, the upper flight of the staircase. The house is presently owned by H. Furlong and Mary Eyre Baldwin.

C23 **Hungars Church** *1742-51; 1840; 1851; 1922; 1950; 1955   Northampton Co. (Just off Route 622 at its junction with Route 619)*

The history of Hungars Church is a history of change. It began as the longest (92 feet) and second largest church in colonial Virginia. Repaired in 1840, it lost its west gable in 1851 and was shortened to its present length of 74 feet 8 inches. Windows were substituted for the central side doors at that time. The original pulpit has disappeared, as have the original pews, though it is perhaps possible that the present ones may be the original box pews cut down. The cornice, roof and floor probably date from 1922. Lighting and heating changes were made in 1950, and further alterations in 1955. Nevertheless, one authority calls the church "a striking building and one of the prime glories of Virginia's Eastern Shore."

C24 **Mount Airy** *1748-58; 1844; 1965   Richmond Co. (From Tappahannock, 4 miles north on Route 360, left on Route 624, straight ahead through gate) Private*

Built by John Tayloe to replace an earlier house that burned in 1740, the present Mount Airy, in turn, burned in 1844. Although the original stone walls remained, the interiors and the roof were rebuilt by Van Ness. Recently the present owner, Col. Henry Gwynne Tayloe, has modernized the house by installing central heating and a new kitchen in one of the quadrant connectors and by putting the house into good repair.

Mount Airy is one of the few major houses of Virginia executed in stone, rough sandstone trimmed with Aquia Creek stone. Its plan of a central block with quadrant connecting units to the dependencies derives from Palladio, while window enframements, loggias, and even the massing of the central block may be traced back to the English architectural books

C25

C26

C27

112 Architecture in Virginia

used in the colony at that time. Mount Airy, as with many of the Tayloe houses, has a sophistication and an insistence on careful detail not often met with in the mid-Georgian buildings in the State.

C25 **Sabine Hall** *c. 1735; 1764; 1830-40; 1929; c. 1960   Richmond Co. (South from Route 360 just west of Warsaw to Route 624, continue to end of road) Private*

When Landon Carter built Sabine Hall the central block was freestanding, and the original kitchen was detached. Since that time, the kitchen was connected to the house with a covered way (1764), the two porches were added (1764), and the roof was lowered (1764); the house was stuccoed and the kitchen pulled down (1830-40); the west wing was added and the east one enlarged (1929); and both wings have been altered during this decade.

In spite of all these changes it is still possible to sense the original exterior, with its unusual stone features at the entrance on two fronts, and the stone lintels, so seldom used in Virginia, over the windows. But the glory of Sabine Hall is the great entrance hall (18' x 38') with the cross hall at the center for the stairs. Its paneling has survived intact, and its pilasters, splendid entablature and the curious construction of the staircase itself make one of the most superb architectural documents in the country. The present owners of this important early-Georgian house are Mr. Robert Carter Wellford and the Rev. and Mrs. Dabney Wellford.

C26 **Aquia Church** *1751-57   Stafford Co. (Three miles north of Stafford Courthouse, turn right at sign on Route 11) Scheduled services*

Although services had been held on or near this site since 1654, an inscription on this church for Overwharton Parish says, "Built A.D. 1751. Destroyed by fire 1754 and rebuilt A.D. 1757 by Mourning Richards, Undertaker: Wm. Copein, Mason." The walls survived the 1754 fire, but the roof and interior were rebuilt. Copein took advantage of the local supply of sandstone for the beautiful enframements of the doors and for the quoins. Aquia Church is one of two colonial churches in Virginia with a true Greek cross plan; its little tower is most unusual; and its interior, with its rich, triple-tiered pulpit, its classical reredos, its square pews and its handsome balconies, is one of the most elaborate in the Commonwealth. Although extensive repairs have been made at various times, Aquia Church has survived largely unchanged.

C27 **Stratford** *1725; 1800   Westmoreland Co. (40 miles east of Fredericksburg on Route 3, left on Route 214 for 2 miles to entrance) Daily except Christmas, 9-4:30   Fee*

This wonderful H-shaped, early Georgian house has triumphantly survived time and many changes. Built by Thomas Lee, it underwent drastic remodeling during the time Lighthorse Harry Lee owned it. By 1800 he had removed or replaced all the exterior stairs and changed all the interiors ex-

C28

C29

cept the Great Hall. When the Robert E. Lee Memorial Foundation bought Stratford in 1929, the task of restoration began. The foundation and the balusters for the central exterior stairs were found. The library, library closet, dining room and dining-room closet were restored, but the corridors, parlor, Lee's birth room and the adjoining bedroom were left in their 1800 state. Seven of the original twelve outbuildings were standing in 1929, and all will eventually be restored.

Stratford has always been one of the most important houses in Virginia. Its formal site plan, with the four brick dependencies so carefully placed at the four corners of a square surrounding the house, its sturdy character, its Palladian use of an upper level for major rooms, its massed chimneys, its relation to the river and its beautiful central hall, with its pilastered paneling and tray ceiling, make of it an exceptional architectural accomplishment in a colony that was just over a century old. Although the solution of the problem of two approaches, by land and by water, gives balance to a careful design, no documented architect may be assigned to Stratford.

C28 **Yeocomico Church** *1706; 1906; 1939-49   Westmoreland Co. (From Warsaw, 3 miles north on Route 3 to Lyells, right on 203 for 5½ miles to Griffen's Corner, left on Route 604 for 3½ miles, left on Route 606 for 1¼ miles to church on left) Scheduled services*

Built first as a wooden church in the 17th century, Yeocomico may or may not have incorporated portions of that earlier building in the present brick structure. Repaired many times in both the 18th and 19th centuries, it was thoroughly restored in 1906 under the supervision of Daniel McCarthy; the present clapboard ceiling, following the lines of the original, was installed in 1939; electricity was installed in 1947; heating, in 1949. One authority points out that it is "perplexing, particularly as to its original shape and masonry," and that the architectural style is a "transistional example—between Gothic and Classical."

In spite of these perplexities, its T-shaped plan, its entrance porch, its interior liturgical arrangements, its original entrance doors with their unique wicket for use in bad weather and its original walnut Holy Table triumph over all the later renewals and changes (such as the windows) and still transmit the feeling of an early and charmingly simple structure.

C29 **Courthouse** *1851-52; 1916; 1926   Fredericksburg (Princess Anne and George Sts.) Mon.-Fri., 9-4; Sat., 9-12*

Designed by James Renwick, the New York architect, this Gothic Revival courthouse replaced an earlier building of 1733, which was demolished to make way for the newer one. When first erected, its brick was exposed and the roof was shingled. The blurring of the sharp brick outlines by the rough stucco added in 1916 and the substitution of the copper roof in 1926 lessen the early romanticism of the building a little, but one may still perceive the crispness of the original in the elongated windows and the slender bell tower.

C30

C31

C32

C30 **James Monroe Law Office** *c. 1750-1770* *Fredericksburg (908 Charles St.) Daily except Christmas, 9-5 Fee*

This simple office building, which seems to have been built in several stages, was used by James Monroe from 1786, when he began his law practice and his career of public service. It is a functional, logical structure, geared to its needs and stripped of embellishments. It is one of the very few city offices of so early a date to have survived. At present, it is owned by the Commonwealth of Virginia.

C31 **Kenmore** *1752* *Fredericksburg (1201 Washington Ave.) Daily except Jan. 1 and 2 and Dec. 25 and 26; summer, 9-5; winter, 9-4 Fee*

The large but excessively plain exterior of this house effectively shields its rich and atypical interior. To begin with, the central hall has been abandoned, and, indeed, symmetry of plan does not appear at all on the first floor. The principal feature of the house is the elaborate plasterwork of some of the ceilings and overmantels. The design of the library plaster may be traced to a plate in Batty Langley's *City and Country Builders' Treasury*, 1740, and is an example of the influence of English architectural books on American building. Although all of the plasterwork is anonymous, some of it was almost certainly executed by the plasterer (called "that Frenchman") who worked for George Washington. Fielding Lewis, who built Kenmore, was Washington's brother-in-law. The design of the house is attributed to the rather shadowy figure John Ariss, but its exterior is so simple, and even old fashioned for its date, that one wonders if a professional designer had worked with Col. Lewis at all.

The house has had an interesting history of restoration. Threatened in 1922, it was saved by the then newly organized Kenmore Association. The Association removed the post-Civil War changes and rebuilt in brick on the early foundations the dependencies, which were originally wood. The Garden Club of Virginia restored its garden in 1929, the first such project to be undertaken by this group.

C32 **National Bank of Fredericksburg** *1820* *Fredericksburg (900 Princess Anne St.) Banking hours*

The Farmers' Bank of Virginia built this banking house and cashier's residence in the Federal style, which allowed, within its simple terms, great expressiveness in detail, clearly seen, for example, in the differences between the public door to the banking rooms, with its engaged, pedestaled columns and full entablature, and the private entrance on the side, with its semi-elliptical fan light. The insurance policy of March 4, 1820, was written for a value of $13,650 to cover the banking and dwelling quarters of two stories and a separate kitchen and meat house. Ruined in 1865, the Farmers' Bank of Virginia, which had branches in Alexandria, Danville, Petersburg, Richmond and Fredericksburg, sold its premises to the National Bank of Fredericksburg, which has preserved the banking equipment, and only after 1920 turned the cashier's quarters into offices.

C33

C33 **Old Stone Warehouse** *1727   Fredericksburg (William & Sophia Sts.)*

This simple building is a forceful example of the architectural effect possible through the straightforward use of materials. It is thought to be the earliest masonry building in Fredericksburg, to have been used as jail, warehouse and slave quarters, and its stone walls, small openings and slate roof make a positive statement that contrasts sharply with many of our present-day commercial and governmental buildings.

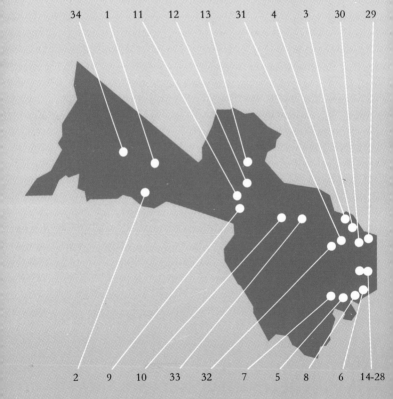

Northern Virginia is as remarkable for its early and its recent planned towns as for any other architectural feature, beautiful and famous as some of these other features are. Alexandria, authorized and laid out in 1749, was established at the site of an existing and well-known tobacco warehouse, and, after an incredibly short space of time, it became the third ranking seaport in the New World. About 1760 it was described as "a small trading place in one of the finest situations imaginable. The Potomac above and below the town is not more than a mile broad, but it here opens into a large circular bay of at least twice that diameter. The town is built upon an arc of this bay; at one extremity of which is a wharf; at the other a dock for building ships; with water sufficiently deep to launch a vessel of any rate or magnitude."

Reston, the new city being built at the present time near Dulles Airport, has been conceived with as much care as Alexandria, and designed even more carefully. It is, however, entirely of its time and takes intelligent advantage of all the progress made in sociology, economics and building during the intervening centuries. Old Alexandria and new Reston, then, give us superb examples of city planning at two very different times in our nation's history.

Alexandria, ca. 1855

D1

D2

D3

D₁ **Annefield** *c. 1790   Clarke Co. (From Berryville, south on Route 340, right on Route 633, one mile) Private*

A little old-fashioned for its date, Annefield substitutes the stone native to its location for the brick of the Tidewater area of the State. One should note that even the broad flight of steps leading to the portico is also built of rough-dressed field stone. The wood trim, however, is light in proportion and as finely detailed as that of any Federal building of the period. Its interiors, in which the original floors and hardware have survived, are very fine indeed. The present owner is Mr. William Bell Watkins.

D₂ **Long Branch** *1811-12; c. 1845; c. 1950 (?)   Clarke Co. (From White Post, east on Route 628, left on Route 626 for 1 mile to entrance on right) Private*

Benjamin Henry Latrobe sent plans for Long Branch to Robert Carter Burwell in 1811 after a six months' correspondence, though it is assumed that Burwell's builder had already begun work on the foundations, for Latrobe was writing in July, "How far are you advanced? . . . Is it possible to modify your plan . . . I will immediately take it regularly in hand." It is a little difficult to know precisely what Latrobe's contribution to this marvelous neo-classic house was, for not only was he working with an existing foundation but later, c. 1845, the interior was re-trimmed in the Minard Lafever manner, the present staircase was installed, and the loggia of the wing was enclosed. The present owner, Mr. Abram Stevens Hewitt, added a study (on the foundations of the old kitchen) and the unit connecting it to the main house.

Latrobe did add the service staircase, for he wrote Burwell that the "great fault of your plan is want of private communication for your family . . . Your only staircase fronts the external door . . . Not a vessel, or nurse or servant can approach but through the hall."

The house, even in its altered state, is exceptionally interesting, with its hip roof crowned by the rectangular belvedere, its two porticoes, the one Greek Ionic and the other Roman Doric, and its beautiful spiral stairs. At least one original mantel by Tranquair of Philadelphia has survived. Talbot Hamlin, the biographer of Latrobe, says that Long Branch "as one of the few existing houses Latrobe is known to have designed, is an important monument in American architecture."

D₃ **Faulkner House** *1964   Fairfax Co. (1151 Crest Lane, McLean: north off Route 123 on Crest Lane, immediately east of interchange with George Washington Parkway; take second right opposite mailbox) Private*

Built for and designed by Avery C. Faulkner, this extraordinary house is the result of the architect's feeling that it is impossible to ignore the past, from which much may be learned. The sense of balance, geometry and formality in the house all stem from this background. But the architect's intelligence must be

D4

D5

D6

credited for the dramatic use of the site and view, as well as the precise contemporary forms the above qualities have taken in the house.

D4 **George Washington Memorial Parkway** *1930-32 Fairfax Co.*

Envisioned as early as 1872 and revived in the 1901 study of the McMillan Commission, the George Washington Memorial Parkway is the direct result of the Capper-Cramton Act of 1930, which, in turn, was based on the 1927 report of Charles W. Eliot, City Planner and Director of Planning for the National Capital Park and Planning Commission. The first portion, the Mount Vernon Memorial Highway, constructed by the Bureau of Public Roads, was completed as a project of the George Washington Bicentennial Celebration. The road is to extend, in Virginia, from Mount Vernon to Great Falls, and, in Maryland, from Ft. Washington to Great Falls, thus protecting both banks of the Potomac. Each detail of the road has been carefully executed, so that it becomes a splendid fusion of engineering, design and landscape architecture.

D5 **Gunston Hall** *1755-58 Fairfax Co. (From Washington, Route 95, Lorton exit, follow signs) Daily except Christmas, 9:30-5 Fee*

When George Mason built Gunston Hall, he had the good fortune to have, as an indentured workman, William Buckland, the the carver, joiner and (at a somewhat later period) architect. The indenture papers for this very superior workman have survived, and in Mason's endorsement on them it is stated that Buckland had executed all the woodwork in the house.

The house itself is a simple, transitional story-and-a-half structure, given importance only by its quoins and its porches. Its interiors are what give it distinction, especially those of its two principal rooms, one Chinese Chippendale in manner and the other Palladian. Both are carefully and lovingly executed and are obviously the work of a young man anxious to demonstrate his skills. Fortunately, Buckland's skills were considerable, and the ideas he brought from England were fresh and up to date.

The house is now owned by the Commonwealth of Virginia, but is administered by the Gunston Hall Board of Regents of the National Society of the Colonial Dames.

D6 **Mount Vernon** *1735-39 (?); c. 1759; 1773-81; 1785 Fairfax Co. (Mount Vernon Memorial Highway) Daily, March 1-Oct. 31, 9-5; Nov. 1-Feb. 28, 9-4:30*

The first house at Mount Vernon was probably built by Augustine, the father of George Washington. On the death of Augustine in 1743, the estate came into the possession of Lawrence, brother of George. Lawrence died in 1752, and George Washington bought his sister-in-law's interest in Mount Vernon at that time. The house in 1752 was a story and a half high, with a central hall and four small rooms on the first floor. The house was first enlarged by being raised to two and a half stories before Washington's marriage in 1759, the work being supervised by William Fairfax of Belvoir.

D6

D7

126 Architecture in Virginia

In July, 1774, Washington wrote a friend "I am very much engaged in raising one of the additions to my house." This work continued during the war years with Lund Washington supervising the completion of the north and south ends of the mansion, the two dependencies and their connecting colonnades. The piazza was erected in 1785, and the weather vane added in 1787.

Though no architect is recorded for Mount Vernon, it is apparent that there was a unifying guide through the years of its transformation. Otherwise the mansion would not have assumed its Palladian aspect so successfully. One should also look carefully at the beautifully ordered site plan, in which every necessary element of the plantation is made to serve the design. In addition, the two-story piazza seems to have been an innovation, and the rustication of the timber siding and its sanding (to give a stone texture) intensifies the formality of the building.

The interior was finished at various times. The mantel of the dining room dates from 1775, that in the west parlor from perhaps a little earlier. The library was not completed until some time after 1775. The New Room or banquet hall was not finished until 1786, the mantel, called by Washington "too elegant and costly by far," being sent from England by Samuel Vaughan.

Just as Mount Vernon was a major preoccupation of its former owner, so has it become for its present owners, the Mount Vernon Ladies Association of the Union, who rescued it from almost certain ruin just before the Civil War. Their pioneering restoration work has preserved not only a national shrine but an architectural monument of great beauty.

D 7 **Pohick Church** *1769-74; 1840; 1874; 1901-16   Fairfax Co. (From Alexandria, 12 miles South on Route 1) Daily, 9-5*

President Washington and George Mason were both on the vestry at the time of the building of Pohick Church. It is said that Washington drew the south elevation and the plan, while Mason, as executor for Daniel French, the original undertaker (contractor), was involved in its building. William Copein was the mason, and it has been suggested that Col. James Wren may have had a connection with its design, as it is very similar to the churches at Falls Church and Alexandria.

The church was given a new roof and ceiling in 1840, although the exterior cornice may be original; a partial restoration was made in 1874 after the interior had been stripped during the Civil War; and another restoration in 1901-16 resulted in the present interior, of which only the cornice and a single baluster of the chancel rail are original. The present balcony is modern.

The exterior is marked by its stone trim, used more lavishly here than in any other church in the State. But stone was used in other ways as well as in the door enframements and quoins. Copein, the mason, was commissioned to make a stone font "according to a draught in the 150th Plate in Langley's Designs—for the price of six pounds, he finding for himself, everything." It was to be ample for "dipping the Infant in the water

D8

D9

D10

discreetly and warily." French, the undertaker, agreed also "to build two Horse Blocks with each two flights of Steps, and to fix Six Benches for the People to sit on under the Trees."

D8   **Pope-Leighey House** *1940; 1964*   *Fairfax Co. (14 miles from Washington on Route 1) Daily except Christmas, 9:30-4:30*   *Fee*

Saved from destruction by being moved from the path of a new highway, this first of three Frank Lloyd Wright houses in Virginia has been successfully re-sited by its new owners, the National Trust. Built for Mr. and Mrs. Loren Pope, it was an example of what Wright called the "house of moderate cost," a problem he said he "would rather solve with satisfaction to myself and Usonia, than build anything I can think of." Its horizontality, its prototype carport, its walls of three thicknesses of boards fastened together with screws, its built-in furniture, and the elimination of paint by the use of cypress all contribute to this concept. The task of rebuilding the house was made easier by the simplicity of its original structural system. But one should also note that the excitements of the house are derived from the manipulation of light, both natural and artificial, and from the definition of space through architecture.

D9   **Aldie Mill** *c. 1790-1800*   *Loudoun Co. (On Route 50 in Aldie) Work days, 9-5*

This sturdy mill not only served the surrounding farms but served as the nucleus of the town of Aldie, which was founded around it in 1810 on the Little River Turnpike (now Route 50), the earliest private chartered road in Virginia (1796). Thus it had economic, planning and architectural importance.

The mill itself, established by Col. Charles Fenton Mercer, was built by the Colonel's slaves of hand-hewn, chamfered beams, chestnut door frames and home-fired brick. There were twin, overshot wheels and imported burrstones of French flint. Operating today, but not grinding, the building and the business are in the hands of Mr. James E. Douglas, great-great-grandson of the early miller.

D10   **Dulles Airport** *1961-62*   *Loudoun Co. (From Washington, exit 12 from Beltway 495, Dulles Airport Access Road, follow signs*

Eero Saarinen, the designer of Dulles Airport, conceived the idea here of bringing the passenger to the plane in mobile lounges instead of the plane to the passenger as in his TWA terminal at Kennedy International Airport. Thus, he was free of the long, finger-like extensions so frequently used at air terminals, and the passenger was at last given a position of importance in an airport scheme. The resultant ease of circulation from car to plane is miraculous.

But Saarinen did not stop there. He clothed his scheme in a brilliantly airy enclosure with a catenary roof supported on a series of giant columns. The entire complex was set in 9600 acres of former farmland, and its road system, runways, parking spaces and planting have been as carefully designed as the building itself.

D11

D12

D13

D11 **Oak Hill** *1821; 1870's; 1922; 1949   Loudoun Co. (2 miles north of Gilbert's Corner on Route 15) Private*

Built for James Monroe, Oak Hill has been much changed since 1821. In the 1870's its interior was somewhat altered (perhaps the stair was moved at this time), and the iron railing on the principal portico was probably added then. In 1922 the then owner, Frank C. Littleton, enlarged the wings both laterally and vertically, concealing the new second story by setting it back from the outer walls. Between 1924 and 1927 he laid out the gardens and changed some of the interior woodwork. In 1949 the library paneling, designed by Francis C. Almirall, was put in. Although these changes have made it difficult to "see" the original Oak Hill, it is still a most interesting building, with its high ceilings, its noncommittal, almost urban entrance façade and its more rural major portico, which accepts so graciously the non-classic feature of a column in the center. The present owner is Mrs. Thomas N. DeLashmutt.

D12 **Oatlands** *1800-03; 1827; 1910   Loudoun Co. (From Leesburg, 6 miles south on Route 15, left at sign) April-Oct., 10-5   Fee*

Oatlands, built by George Carter, did not receive its portico until 1827. The bricks were made on the estate, and the wood was taken from the surrounding forests. The columns and capitals of the portico were executed by Henry Farnham of New York, shipped to Alexandria, and then brought to Oatlands overland. The plan is most unusual, for the staircases are in the projecting semi-octagonal bays. The porch at the rear was added in 1910, and the gardens were enlarged then and subsequently. This unusually well-documented house is now the property of the National Trust.

D13 **Waterford** *18th & 19th centuries   Loudoun Co. (Route 7 northwest through Leesburg to the junction of Waterford Road, right again to Waterford) Waterford Mill, Sat.-Sun., June-Sept., 1-5; various buildings open during Waterford Weekend, Oct.; inquire Waterford Foundation*

Though Waterford was established as early as 1740, when Amos Janney built a mill, a miller's house, a smithy and a log house, it was not incorporated as a town until 1810. It has survived in a largely unspoiled condition, and is today a fine example of a Virginia village that has escaped industrialization, but is both prosperous and well cared for. There are many lessons to be learned from a walk about the town, not the least of which is the ease with which a great variety of building materials was used, including stone, brick, wood and logs. Of the individual buildings to be noticed, one might mention the mill, a brick structure of c. 1750; the Arch House Row, also of c. 1750, with its charming mixture of stone, brick and wood; the Camelot School of 1800, a two-story log building that had once been weatherboarded; the Baptist church of 1850, a crisp neo-classic building; and the Presbyterian church, rebuilt in 1882 in a more romantic Victorian manner.

D14

D15

D16

D 14 **Agudas Achim Congregation Center** *1958; 1966 Alexandria (2908 Valley Dr.) Mon.-Fri., 9-5*

The clear rectangularity of this synagogue, designed by Miller and Chapman, blends remarkably well with its wooded site. The delicacy of its use of steel gives it a sharp clarity of form so often lacking in contemporary building. One is never lost in such a complex building, and whenever changes of materials occur logic has always been the governing factor. In 1966 it was necessary to add a new library and kitchen by Harold Adler.

D 15 **Carlyle House** *1752; early 19th century Alexandria (121 North Fairfax St., entrance through Carlyle Apartments) Daily except Christmas, 10-5 Fee*

Presumably a part of a larger establishment (with attached dependencies), the Carlyle house was built by John Carlyle, who was also one of the builders of Christ Church. It now finds itself surrounded by the Carlyle Apartment and Office Building and quite changed from its early appearance. Its brick has been stuccoed; its stone quoins are deteriorating; its roof and dormers are probably 19th century; and its entrance door is also early 19th or very late 18th century. Its garden used to extend to the river, but is now bounded by Lee Street. Two of the original rooms have retained their paneling, that of the Blue room being especially rich though not always properly realized architecturally. The house is important, however, for it shows an early domestic use of quoins, a device very well liked in this area. The present owner is Mr. Lloyd Diehl Schaeffer.

D 16 **Christ Church** *1767-73; 1785-c. 1818 Alexandria (Cameron & N. Washington Sts.) Weekdays, 9-5; Sun., 2-5*

As it is known that a James Wren presented plans in 1767 for Christ Church, as well as for Falls Church, they become two of the few colonial churches for which a definite designer may be assigned. James Parsons served as the first contractor, but was unable to finish the building. The first contract was for £600, but the Vestry gave a second contract for £220 to John Carlyle, and the church was accepted as "finished in workman-like order" on February 27, 1773. Although the two tiers of windows were original, indicating the intention to have a balcony, none was added until some time between 1785 and 1818. This latter date saw the addition of the tower, although it would seem there have been later additions to it. The original rectangular, hip-roofed building is handsomely trimmed in Aquia Creek stone, which is now painted.

The interior of this church, though splendid, is far from being original, the chief survival being the tablets on either side of the pulpit, which were lettered by James Wren, and which are untouched. We have already seen that the balconies are a later addition. It is thought that neither the pulpit nor the communion rail is original; the floor of the aisles has been raised; and there is some controversy over the original arrangement of the pews.

D17

D18

D19

D20

D17 **Downtown Baptist Church** *c. 1830; 1858-59* *Alexandria (212 S. Washington St.) Open for services*

Built first c. 1830, and undergoing major repairs in 1858-59, this church is an example of the 19th century device of raising the principal floor of a church a story above the entrance level so that the ground floor may be used for other purposes, usually for Sunday School. The exaggerated point of the spire seems to be the one luxuriant design feature of the building, which otherwise makes its effect through mass and proportion and the repetition of blind arcading, at the cornice and as a relief for the face of the nave balcony.

D18 **Dulaney House** *1783; c. 1800-10* *Alexandria (601 Duke St.) Private*

Built as a town house by Benjamin Dulaney, whose country place was on Shuter's Hill overlooking Alexandria, this building is notable for its restraint, and it is already beginning to show the fineness and simplicity of Federal design as opposed to that of the colonial Georgian. Soon after 1800 its detached kitchen was connected to the house by a two-story bridge, and the entrance door was also changed at that time. The garden has been newly designed, and the dining room has been re-paneled by the present owners, Mr. and Mrs. John Howard Joynt.

D19 **Fairfax House** *c. 1752; c. 1782; c. 1800; 1929* *Alexandria (207 Prince St.) Private*

Of the 18th century houses left standing in the 200 block of Prince Street, perhaps the most interesting is the George William Fairfax house. Its fourteen owners have changed it from its mid-18th century square shape. Although it is uncertain whether it was first built before or after 1752, when the lot was transferred from William Fairfax to his son George William, it is known that a wing was added before 1782. The front door, the stairway, the mantels and much of the woodwork were changed about 1800. The chimneys and dormers were blown down in 1927 and replaced in 1929. We find, then, that though the house was begun quite early, it now has a very strong Federal air. This evolution of styles within a single building makes a fascinating study of the house, which is now the property of Mrs. Charles Beatty Moore.

D20 **Gadsby's Tavern** *1752; 1792; 1949* *Alexandria (Royal & Cameron Sts.) Daily, May-Oct., 10-5 Fee*

The earlier coffee house, built in 1752, and the later tavern, built in 1792 for John Wise, make up one of the more elaborate 18th century hostelries not only in Virginia but in the country. The Metropolitan Museum bought the ballroom paneling and front door of the tavern. The ballroom has been installed in the museum's American Wing, but the door was returned to Alexandria in 1949. All the interiors, including the ballroom, have been restored, and well demonstrate the considerable elegance that it was possible to achieve in a public house in the

D21

D22

D23

young nation. Post 24 of the American Legion owns the coffee house and tavern now, an appropriate owner, as it was often used for military activities during its early days.

D21 **Goodman House** *1954* *Alexandria (514 N. Quaker Lane) Private*

Charles Goodman, discovering that the old house he had bought only for the land on which it stood was very solid indeed, spent five years in it before remodeling it or adding to it. When, as architect, he did bring it up to date he retained its boxy character, reserving the transparency possible through modern technology for the addition. He also added a terrace for each season to this new living room wing, so that the outdoors might be experienced from within the room or from outside. The success of the scheme demonstrates once more the value of thought in architecture.

D22 **Hollin Hills** *1949-62* *Alexandria (1223 Fort Hunt Rd.; Route 1 south to Fort Hunt Rd., left just past Beltway) By appointment*

Hollin Hills is a development based on ideas and imagination, and its many awards, including its exhibition as one of the "10 Milestones in the Future of America's Architecture," are demonstrations of the importance of these qualities. Its developer, Robert Davenport, calls his method "a consumer's approach to the housing project." The buyer chooses from fourteen plans developed over the years by the architect, Charles M. Goodman, but the buyer may make changes within the context of the design. Similarly, he must work with the landscape architect, at present Eric Caepcke, who was preceded by Bernard Voight (who originated the scheme of making the "community look as if there were no individual lots but a beautiful park") and Dan Kiley. In this way the buyer is able to fit his desired scheme into the grand design.

The development began with 236 acres but now has 326, of which a considerable proportion is given over to park land and buffer areas of woods between Hollin Hills and other developments. There are now 400 houses finished, and the project will be completed in 1969 when the total has reached 450.

Mr. Goodman has always regarded Hollin Hills as an experimental station where "every change in family needs was expressed in the next design. This was the fundamental tenet along with the desire to get away from straight historical reproduction." He wanted his buildings to "stay alive and to have a relationship to each other while being made to fit the individual site. One of the major aims of the project was to secure the participation of the owner."

This collaboration of developer, architect, landscape architect and owner has pointed out an intelligent and successful path for post-war housing all too seldom followed.

D23 **Lee House** *late 1790's; later additions* *Alexandria (428 N. Washington St.) Private*

Started by Beale Howard in the late 1790's but finished by Edmund Jennings Lee, who was living in it by 1801, this house

D24

D25

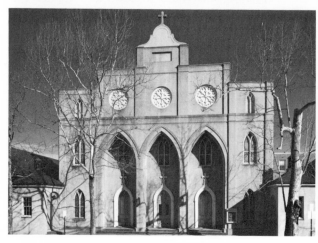

D26

exemplifies the persistence of the Georgian style to quite a late date. Since that time, the two first-floor rooms, which shared a single chimney between them, were thrown into one, with the fireplace being moved to the rear wall; and two additions have been made beyond this chimney, the last addition being fairly recent. The date of the galleried porches is uncertain. The pedimented doorway with its Aquia Creek stone steps and the strong cornice give distinction to this fine town house presently owned by Mr. Edward C. Plyer and Mr. Joseph R. Cipolari.

D24 **Lloyd House** *1793-96; 1960   Alexandria (220 N. Washington St.) Private*

Owned at one time by John Wise, the builder of Gadsby's Tavern, and later by John Lloyd (after 1832), this late-Georgian house has lost its original interiors. In 1960 it was restored by the present owner, Mr. Robert V. New, but its fate is, at the moment, uncertain. The pedimented door would seem to be its principal ornament, but the records are now so inadequate that it is almost impossible to speak of its original condition.

D25 **Old Presbyterian Meeting House** *1774; 1835-37; 1843; 1853   Alexandria (321 S. Fairfax St.) Open daily*

Though first built in 1774, the Presbyterian Meeting House suffered a disastrous fire in 1835. It was rebuilt and ready for services by July 30, 1837. The bell-tower was added in 1843, and the entrance vestibule and steps, in 1853. The original and pre-Revolutionary portions, then, are the south and north walls beyond the vestibule, and the west wall. It is uncertain whether any of the interior was saved and reused. Nevertheless, the simplicity and the clarity of the church have been so well preserved through the various rebuildings that the structure reflects a religious purity not often met with in our smaller churches.

D26 **St. Paul's Church** *1817   Alexandria (Pitt St., north of Duke St.) Open for services*

This interesting Gothic Revival church was sadly changed from Benjamin Henry Latrobe's designs while it was being built. On August 10, 1817, he wrote the rector that he had "given you the best design which I could find on the foundations for your church . . . I now find . . . that not only is the whole church lowered eighteen inches, but square windows are put in the flanks. What a confession of ostentatious poverty! The congregation are proud enough to build a handsome front to show . . . but too poor to be consistent in the flanks, & too inconsistent in their opinion of their architect, whether of his honesty or skill, I will not pretend to say, to believe that he is capable of judging as correctly respecting the body of a church as of its front . . ." The rector's reply was not satisfactory to Latrobe, for he wrote again on August 16 that his object was "by strong language first to make an impression that should rescue your building from just criticism, & then to prove that the only plea in favor of the change was not well founded, & that my plan was the most economical . . ."

D27

D28

D29

In spite of the "just criticism" and in spite of the exterior being described today as "Spanish Mission," there are many fascinating and even dramatic features to be found in this example of Latrobe's Gothic style.

D27 **Vowell-Smith House** *1840 (?)* *Alexandria* (*510 Wolfe St.*) *By appointment*

Mr. Vowell built twin houses for his two daughters. One of them married a Col. Smith and lived in this, the surviving house of the pair. Its rather plain exterior (for a Victorian building), is not much of a preparation for the rich interiors, with their fourteen foot ceilings, heavy plaster ornamentation, chandeliers and the thirteen black or white marble fireplaces. The white marble mantels are charming, with their vines heavy with ripened grapes or fruit baskets overflowing with luscious apples and pears. Though the coach house and the servants' wing have been turned into apartments, the house still sits in a large garden surrounded by its original iron fence. Mrs. Zerelda C. McConnell is its owner.

D28 **Warehouses** *late 18th & 19th centuries* *Alexandria* (*King St.*) *Some open in business hours*

Alexandria still has a remarkable group of commercial buildings in the early warehouses on King Street. Perhaps the earliest of these is John Fitzgerald's warehouse, built in 1765 by John Paterson, at 6 King Street. The Chequire and the Gilpin houses at 202 and 206-208 King Street, dating from the end of the 18th or the first of the 19th centuries, contained offices at ground level and the merchant's residence above. The Chequire house still has its plaster cornices and a decorated ceiling in the upper rooms. There are also later 19th century warehouses to be seen here. A movement to rehabilitate these old and simple structures is underway.

D29 **Arlington (Custis-Lee Mansion)** *1802-18* *Arlington National Cemetery Daily, Oct. 1-March 31, 9:30-4:30; April 1-Sept. 30, 9:30-6*

Started in 1802, only the two wings of Arlington were finished at the time of the wedding of George Washington Parke Custis in 1804. He and his wife lived in the north wing while they entertained visitors in the south wing. The great Doric portico and the central portion of the house were finished in 1818. In 1859, when Robert E. Lee insured it after his father-in-law's death, he stated that "the Mansion House is covered with Slate and the wings with gravel . . . The division walls are of brick." He valued the mansion at $20,000 but insured it for only $5,000.

Arlington's splendid, heavy portico is strong enough to make its point at the top of the bluff above the Potomac. Even today it dominates Washington in spite of the city's metropolitan growth. But today's viewer should remember that the stucco on the brick columns was originally painted to represent marble, as old photographs show. The interior of Arlington is more Federal than Greek Revival, and its delicacy of woodwork is in marked contrast to the sturdiness of the portico.

D30

D31

D32

D33

D30 **Unitarian Church** *1964 Arlington (4444 Arlington Blvd.) Open for services*

Designed by Charles M. Goodman as a "great meeting room," with the intent of making the congregation feel like strong individuals as well as part of a deeper unity, this church expresses that intent extraordinarily well. The high windows, the strong emphasis on structure and the throwing of the interior space into a single volume help to achieve this desired result. Variety is given by the slightly asymmetrical placement of the interior furnishing and the location of the balcony. Order brings unity and order is a fundamental of this building.

D31 **Falls Church** *1767-69; 1823-39; 1865; 1905; 1959 Falls Church (E. Fairfax & N. Washington Sts.) Weekdays, 9-5*

The Vestry records of Falls Church state that on March 28, 1763, "the church is greatly in decay and want of repairs—it should be replaced—that a new church be built at the same place." George Washington was one of the Vestrymen at this meeting and was one of the Wardens for the following year. Col. James Wren designed the church, which has the present molded brick west door, but originally had a stone doorway on the south, which would have increased the distinction of the church. The walls, except for repairs, are original, as are many of the upper windows and perhaps the cornice. After a period of neglect the church was renewed in the early 19th century; again after the Civil War with help from the federal government; again in 1905; and finally in 1959, when the addition of a new chancel was built, and the old church became only the nave. Practically nothing remains of the old interior.

D32 **Fountain of Faith** *1952 Falls Church (Route 29-211, west of Falls Church)*

This beautiful fountain by Carl Milles is the focal point of the National Memorial Park, a cemetery handsomely designed with a grand axial plan. The proprietors of the Park commissioned the fountain to express the "warmth and tenderness, the joy and strength of supreme love in all human relationships . . ." Milles once more triumphed in this grouping of many figures and many jets of water, achieving a subtle interplay of forms and a mystery through his juxtaposition of the motionless bronze and the flowing water. The Fountain of Faith is, without doubt, one of the nation's greatest fountains.

D33 **Reston** *1965 Fairfax Co. (18 miles west of Washington, four miles east of Dulles Airport; may be reached by Airport Access Highway)*

Reston, the creation of Robert E. Simon, Jr., is a new town that eventually will house 75,000. It is to have a series of neighborhood centers, as well as a larger town center. It is designed for the individual and to free the individual from the difficulties of commuting. Its master plan was drawn up by Whittlesey, Conklin and Rossant. The buildings to the left as one looks at the lake from the square in the first neighborhood were de-

D34

signed by Mr. Conklin, those to the right by Chloethiel Wood-
ard Smith, and those in the woods above the lake are by Charles
M. Goodman. Those around the golf course are by Louis Sauer.
All these groups of buildings are at a miraculously high level
of achievement.

Lake Anne Village Center was opened with the sound of bells
and amid music, plays and poetry readings. As August Heck-
scher pointed out in his dedicatory address, the "true community cannot exist without experiences which give delight to
the spirit." Mr. Simon has certainly provided those experiences
architecturally with his imaginative direction of Reston, which
may well become the prototype for the solution of the urban
ills of the rest of the nation.

D34 **Handley Library** *1908-13*   *Winchester* (*Braddock & Piccadilly Sts.*)
Mon.-Fri., 10-5

This rich example of the Beaux-Arts manner was designed by J.
Stewart Barney and Henry Otis Chapman of New York. Working drawings and specifications for it have survived. Its materials included Indiana limestone, native limestone, James
River granite, hollow floor tiles, and partition blocks of hard-
burnt clay. It was a remarkably advanced building not only in
its facilities, which included five floors of stacks with glass floors
for the admission of light and a lecture room in the basement,
but also in its having been built to be fireproof. There have
been few changes except for a basement room and a necessary
protective platform in the dome. The sophisticated forms, the
rich materials and the generous planning of this library make
it an unusual monument of the early 20th century in the State.

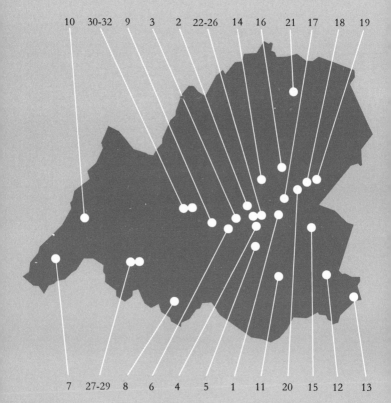

Section E The Piedmont Area Introduction

The area to the west of Richmond, with a few exceptions such as Tuckahoe, reached the peak of its early architectural development during the post-Revolutionary years. Thomas Jefferson was the towering architectural influence here during the early years of the Republic, and his own architectural activities were climaxed by his buildings for the University of Virginia. But he (and indeed the entire area) was plagued by incompetent workmen. Even constant supervision failed to eliminate the provincialisms perpetrated by the insufficiently trained craftsmen. This improper execution weakened the monumentality but strengthened the humanism of the new columnar, neo-classic buildings.

As one continues west, this difficulty becomes more and more apparent, and especially is it true of the farms one sees along the roads of the Valley. An informality unknown to the plantation houses of the east is seen, and even the more important buildings are sometimes a little lax in their use of classical elements. But the 20th century has countered this shortcoming of the area with the superb design of the Skyline Drive, with many extraordinarily handsome country houses and with several of the recently erected public schools.

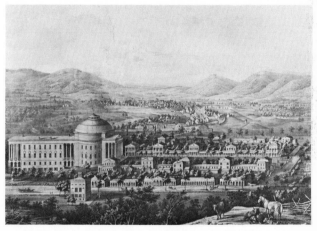

Bohn's "View of the University of Virginia, Charlottesville and Monticello taken from Lewis Mountain," 1856

E1

E2

E3

E4

E₁ **Castle Hill** *1764; 1824; 1947   Albemarle Co. (from Charlottesville, east on Route 250, left on Route 22 to Route 231, north on Route 231 for 4 miles beyond Cismont) Private*

Castle Hill is a remarkable house in that its two major periods of building produced two equally fine but very different parts, which combine into a most harmonious whole. The earlier, 18th century portion, built for Dr. Thomas Walker, with its steep roof and sharp dormers, is typical of the less grand domestic building of the time. The early 19th century portion, built for William Cabell Rives, with its high ceilings and large windows, brings both sophistication and expansiveness to the plantation. Its box-bordered drive to the east and bowling green to the west give splendid foregrounds to the handsome but contrasting views, while remnants of the plantation streets survive on either side. The house was brought into condition in 1947 and is presently owned by Mrs. Clark J. Lawrence.

E₂ **Farmington** *1802; 1929   Albemarle Co. (From Charlottesville, west 2 miles on Route 250, right at club sign) 7:30-10*

Built for George Divers, but burned out during the mid-19th century, the front, or Jeffersonian, portion of Farmington was transformed into a single, large, two-storied room when the house became Farmington Country Club in 1929. Nevertheless, the portico and the semi-octagonal ends of the building give some sense of its original look. What is especially interesting is the evidence of Jefferson's forced reliance on workmen who were not very knowledgeable, evidence to be found in the awkwardness of the capitals, which are too small for the columns of the pedimented portico. The bull's eye windows above the tall, floor-length windows of the first floor are other unchanged features of Jefferson's design.

E₃ **Mirador** *c. 1832   Albemarle Co. (West of Charlottesville, 14 miles on Route 250) Private*

When James M. Bowen built Mirador it was a large but rather simple neo-classic house. Enlarged in this century, it was given very handsome but new interiors and made rather more grandiose than its original builders had intended. At this time, however, a most wonderful garden was laid out. Its transition from formality near the house to the informality of the open fields was as subtle as any garden in the nation. Mirador now belongs to Mr. and Mrs. Lewis F. Marran.

E₄ **Monticello** *1770-1808   Albemarle Co. 8-5*

Because Jefferson gave reality to many of his architectural dreams at Monticello, it is fair to say that it is a romantic house in spite of its classicism. There was almost a continuous building operation here, and as late as the year before his death Jefferson was importing some of the marble facings for his fireplaces. Although the house and its dependencies were based on the theories of Palladio, the design of the house as we now see it is a very personal expression of the desires of its owner and de-

E5

E6

E7

150 Architecture in Virginia

signer, distilled from the many architectural books in his library, from his travels, and from his experience. One might point out that the house, like Jefferson, was revolutionary in its siting, for the top of a mountain presented enormous practical difficulties at that time.

Monticello is now owned and maintained by the Thomas Jefferson Memorial Foundation, which has carefully retained its neo-classic character throughout all the necessary repairs and rebuildings carried out under its supervision.

E₅ **Redlands** *1798   Albemarle Co. (From Charlottesville, south 9 miles on route 20 to Carter's Bridge, left on Route 708) Private*

Redlands, though unassuming on the exterior, is full of surprise and sophistication inside. Its high ceilings, its projecting, shaped drawing room, and its delicate, early-Republican detail make of it an extremely knowing interior. It was built for Robert Carter under the direction of Martin Thacker. Redlands has never been empty, and has never been out of the hands of the builder's descendants. As a consequence it has the indefinable but necessary ambience of a home as opposed to an exhibition house, though, of course, it has undergone many changes in order to keep it habitable. It is presently owned by Mrs. Robert Hill Carter.

E₆ **Rose Hill** *1930   Albemarle Co. (West of Charlottesville, 15 miles on Route 250, left ½ mile on Route 151) Private*

One of the most handsome country houses built in the Commonwealth during this century, Rose Hill is a fine example of the advantages to be gained from a client and architect insisting that each detail should be carefully executed. The architect, William Lawrence Bottomley, showed his power by controlling these details so that they add to the strength of this beautiful neo-Georgian design. The very large garden was worked out with equal care, and, though considerably reduced in scope today, it still serves as the "right" setting for the house, with its quadrant connections to the end pavilions. From the walled entrance court through the central hall to the loggia with its broad view of the mountains is, as one moves from space to space, an emotional experience created and conditioned by the architecture. The house was built for Mrs. William Massie and is now owned by the Society of Mary.

E₇ **Old Humpback Bridge** *1835   Alleghany Co. (Route 60, 3 miles west of Covington)*

The 19th century covered bridge was both a remarkable engineering feat and a remarkable example of craftsmanship in wood. The wooden trusses, worked out by the engineers of the time, were remarkable for their length. The craftsmanship for most of these bridges was so good that they have perished, usually, from neglect rather than use. It is said that even today a covered bridge is both cheaper and sturdier than our steel and concrete structures for the shorter spans. Despite romantic notions, it seems the bridges were covered to protect the wood

E8

E9

E10

of their skeletons. In Virginia the covered bridge has almost disappeared, but a few examples still stand of this practical and, indeed, exploratory use of wood.

Old Humpback is the oldest of the remaining covered bridges, and the only one of its kind in the country. It was built in 1835 of hand-hewn oak timbers and locust pins, and rises eight feet in the center. Since 1929 it has been used only for foot traffic.

E8 **Sweet Briar House** *c. 1790-1800; 1851-52   Sweet Briar College, Amherst Co. (13 miles north of Lynchburg on Route 29) Private*

Sweet Briar House began as a T-shaped, six-roomed farm house, purchased by Elijah Fletcher, the father of the founder of Sweet Briar College, in 1830. After the return of his daughters from Europe, he enlarged and transformed the house by adding the towers and modifying the existing portico. The result is a pleasing, though provincial, Italianate Victorian house, probably designed by Fletcher and a master builder. All the elements of the mid-19th century romantic classicism are present, while the slight distortions caused by the designers' lack of knowledge add to its nostalgia. Sweet Briar House now serves as a residence for the president of Sweet Briar College, and still contains many of the original furnishings.

E9 **Swannanoa** *1912   Augusta Co. (Turn on Route 610 at the junction of Route 250 and the Skyline Drive, 4 miles east of Waynesboro) Daily: summer, 8-6; winter, 9-5   Fee*

High on a mountainside overlooking a magnificent view of the Shenandoah and Rockfish valleys, Major James Dooley of Richmond built this Florentine villa for his wife, who is immortalized in a huge Tiffany stained glass window on the landing of the double staircase at one end of the very large central hall. The exterior is of Georgia marble and the interior is finished in Italian marbles, oak paneling or with damask stretched on the walls. The elaborately terraced and balustraded gardens with their many pergolas complete the Florentine (and Edwardian) fantasy. The building and its surrounding acreage are now owned by the University of Science and Philosophy.

E10 **Warm Springs Bath Houses** *Men's, 1761; Women's, 1836   Bath Co. (Route 220, 5 miles northeast of Hot Springs) Daily, 9-5 Bath, $1*

The Indians believed these mineral pools were discovered by an exhausted runner whose strength was renewed after a bath in them. By 1761, when the now destroyed Warm Springs Hotel built the men's octagonal bath house (on the right of the photograph), the old Virginia habit of a summer tour of the various springs was well enough established to make such a structure feasible. Both it and the polygonal women's bath house, with its twenty sides, have survived with very little alteration and are excellent examples of the simplicity in public accommodations the early Virginian found once he left home. Now owned by the Homestead Hotel, the buildings are kept in repair and are used for their original purpose.

E11

E12

E13

E11 **Bremo** *1820 Fluvanna Co. (From Richmond, Route 250 west to Zion X-Roads, left on Route 15 to private road on right, beyond Bremo Bluff) Private*

When Gen. John Cocke approached the building of his new house, Bremo, he sought the advice of a number of friends and professionals. Although Thomas Jefferson and a Richmond architect named Conneley were among these, it was John Neilson, a master carpenter, who served as final architect, pulling together all the ideas and sketches that Gen. Cocke had received or had drawn himself. He, too, apparently, was the one who gave the house its noble, Palladian proportions, as all the drawings by others show it with very awkward massing.

The central house, with connecting links and long subsidiary wings, sits the crest of its hill overlooking the James River with what can only be described as grandeur, a word often used in architectural texts of the late 18th and early 19th centuries.

In contrast to the red brick and white trim of the house, the barn was built of very rough field stone. It was given architectural importance, however, by the portico, with its astonishingly sophisticated columns of dry masonry (now strengthened with mortar). The house is still owned by Gen. Cocke's family, the present owner being Mr. Joseph Forney Johnston.

E12 **Courthouse** *1826 Goochland Co. (Route 6) Check Clerk's office for open hours*

Started during the year of Thomas Jefferson's death, this beautiful temple-form courthouse is thought to have been influenced by his pavilions at the University of Virginia. Edward Scott and James Shelton were the probable builder-designers. Certainly the building is very Jeffersonian in feeling and detail, and it is interesting to see that the Roman detail is more correct than that in some of Jefferson's own buildings. Until 1966, when additions were begun, the courthouse complex was a good example of what was needed in a country county seat, for the Clerk's office (1826) and jail (1848), together with the courthouse itself, made a charming group within the large area, which was walled to keep out cattle.

E13 **Tuckahoe** *1712-30 Goochland Co. (From Route 6 west of Richmond, left on County Route 650 2½ miles) Private*

An H-shaped house, Tuckahoe is especially noted for the carving of its two staircases, for the paneling of its central room, and for its very heavy timber framing of the roof. These and its extensive use of weather boarding were only possible in a well-wooded area, and reflect the great skills the builders used with their local materials. It has not been possible to date with any degree of certainty the order of building of the two wings, the one with brick end walls and the other entirely of timber.

The importance of the river as a means of communication at that time is shown by the fronting of the house toward it. Tuckahoe is also notable for the disposition of the plantation street as an element in its site plan.

E14

E15

E16

E17

E14 **Courthouse** *1838   Standardsville, Greene Co. (Route 33) Daily, 9-5,*
except when court is in session

Built ten years later than its predecessor in Madison, the
Greene County Courthouse still shows the Jeffersonian influence in its use of brick, wood and stucco, and in its two-story
portico. That portico, with its unusual detailing of triglyphs
inside as well as out, makes it rather more elaborate than the
Madison building. As no documents concerning its erection
have been saved, it is impossible to make an attribution for this
interesting neo-classic structure.

E15 **Byrd Mill** *1740   Louisa Co. (From Louisa, 4 miles south on Route 659,*
right on Route 640, right at fork on Route 649, 2 miles) Daily, 9-5

The high, slightly leaning part of this still working mill is the
portion built in 1740 by a contractor named Byrd, whose mark
may still be found on the beams, for John Garth. Various additions have been made since at unrecorded dates. The present
burrstones are French, also of uncertain date, but the mill, with
its unpainted weather boarding, mill race, mill stones and
water turbines, with their wooden bearings, is one of the very
few pre-Revolutionary commercial buildings still used for its
original purpose. Mr. John Spencer Clinger, the present miller,
and his staff process over 750,000 pounds of grain a year.

E16 **Courthouse** *1828   Madison Co. (Route 29) Weekdays, 9-5*

The Commissioners of Madison County have preserved the
original contract for their sturdy and forthright courthouse.
The principal builder seems to have been Malcolm F. Crawford, who had worked a few years earlier on the University of
Virginia. As he was aided by two other former University
workmen, it is not surprising that the Jeffersonian influence
should be so strong. The Commissioners played their part, too,
for they wrote into the contract that the roof was "to have a
pediment pitch with a Tuscan cornice drawn in proportion to
the height of the building." The sum of this contract was $3600.
The courthouse still serves as a focal point for its very handsome village, which has recently been saved by the construction of a by-pass to relieve the main street of its former burden
of traffic.

E17 **Barboursville** *1790; 1814-22   Barboursville (Route 20 north 16 miles*
from Charlottesville, right on Route 678 just before junction of Routes 20
and 33, ½ mile to entrance) Private

The existing building at Barboursville was erected for Gov.
James Barbour in 1790. The central house, of 1814-22, designed by Thomas Jefferson—his drawings for it are now at the
Massachusetts Historical Society and have recently been dated
1817—was burned out on Christmas Day, 1884. Nevertheless,
the ruins, having escaped demolition, give an excellent idea of
the original house, with its octagonal room projecting into a
Doric portico and its turf ramp leading from the lawn to that
portico. This noble ruin has another interest: it allows one to

E18

E19

E20

see some of the construction methods used, as in the brick columns, which have lost a portion of their stucco covering. It is perhaps possible, also, to gain a better idea of the original scheme from the ruin than it would be had the house survived in a form altered by the inevitable adaptations to contemporary living. The present owners are Mr. and Mrs. C. Francis Smithers.

E18 **Courthouse** *c. 1852-58; 1949   Orange Co. (Main St. and Madison Rd.) Open*

This, the third courthouse for Orange County, is the result of the destruction of the second courthouse to make way for the Orange and Alexandria railway. The porch on the front was originally open on all three sides, but was filled in during 1949 to provide office space. The Italianate character of the building, with its Tuscan tower (somewhat marred by the present solidity of the two ends of the portico), is a splendid example of a favorite mid-Victorian expression worked out quite logically in brick. The quickened rhythm of the two sizes of arches and the exaggerated projection of the tower cornice are notable features of this interesting civic building.

E19 **Mayhurst** *1859; c. 1911   Orange Co. (From Orange, ½ mile east on Route 15) Private*

This delicious Victorian fantasy was built by Col. John Willis, who retained the original name of an earlier house, Howard Place. Later owned by the Crenshaw family, the house was renamed Mayhurst, and the wing to the east was added c. 1911. The vigor of the Victorian imagination is well illustrated here, a vigor certainly not shackled by timidity. The rusticated wooden siding, the bold balusters of the balconies, the heavy brackets supporting the slender cornice and the crispness of the belvedere, with its elaborate finial, are matched in interest by the oval spiral staircase, which ascends into the cupola. An odd structural feature, discovered during some recent repairs by the present owners, Mr. and Mrs. Frank B. Daniel, is that the 18-inch-thick walls are hollow.

E20 **Montpelier** *1760; 1809; 1900-01   Orange Co. (Route 20, 4 miles west of Orange) Private*

Montpelier is an excellent example of a house that grew. The central portion was built in 1760 by James Madison, Sr.; the present portico and two one-story wings were added in 1809 by his son President James Madison; and William Du Pont, the father of the present owner, Mrs. Marion Du Pont Scott, added a second story to the wings and enlarged the house to its present dimensions. Madison's friendship with Jefferson, Dr. William Thornton (designer of the Capitol in Washington) and Benjamin Latrobe has led to various attributions for the 1809 additions. The columns of the portico do have a Jeffersonian air, but that may be due to workmanship rather than design. The delightful little circular temple is said to be a replica of one in Montpelier, France.

E21

E22

E23

E24

E21 **Skyline Drive** *1931-39 Shenandoah National Park Daily except in bad weather Fee*

As early as 1924 a committee reported through Park Service Director Stephen T. Mather to Secretary of the Interior Hubert Work relative to the proposed Shenandoah National Park that "the greatest single feature, however, is a possible sky-line drive along the mountain top . . ."

Work was not begun until 1931, and was carried out in three sections over a length of c.105 miles. Its total cost was $4,572,-184, an unbelievably low figure by today's standards. These 105 miles, carried out under the supervision of Thomas C. Vint, Chief of Design and Construction at the time, are among the most beautiful roadways in the nation. Not only is the succession of views from the seventy-five overlooks breathtaking, but the placement of the road, its guardwalls, and the treatment of the landscape at its sides all make for a most satisfying visual effect. The Drive, in fact, demonstrates the rich rewards of design control exercised over a large area.

E22 **Arcadia** *1960-63 Charlottesville (Old Ivy Rd., Farmington) Private*

Built for a collector of books, Arcadia states its purpose with its central, octagonal, book-lined, domed room. But Arcadia is remarkable in many other ways. It is remarkable that so large an establishment has been worked out on a single level. It is remarkable how much care has been lavished on every detail. It is remarkable in the beauty and rapid establishment of its gardens. And, of course, it is remarkable for the triumphant solution of the difficult problem of putting a dome on a domestic building. Its architect was Frederick D. Nichols, and it is owned by Mr. and Mrs. C. Waller Barrett.

E23 **Buford Junior High School** *1965-66 Charlottesville (9th St., S.W.) School hours*

Charlottesville has recently built two outstanding junior high schools, both by Caudill, Rowlett and Scott in association with Heyward and Llorens. The one illustrated is marvelously adapted to its site and, although rigidly regular, neither repulses the spectator nor falls into the cold trap of classicism. Its honesty of materials, its logic and its scale allow it to fit into a traditional community, while its contemporary forms and planning make no compromise with the past.

E24 **Frankel House** *1952 Charlottesville (2020 Spotswood Rd.) Private*

The Frankel house was a reasoned answer to the critics of modern architectural form at the time it was built, for it demonstrated its ability to settle into an established environment without destroying it. Now it has become a classic, and is regarded with both pride and affection by those who were at first most upset by its flat roof, pierced brick screen and large areas of glass. The brick screen, by the way, was a very early step by the architect, Edward D. Stone, in his later use of architectural screens. The house is owned by Dr. and Mrs. Charles Frankel.

E25

E26

E25 **University Hall, University of Virginia** *1965 Charlottesville* (*Emmett St.*) *Open for public events*

University Hall is a major demonstration of the vitality of the University traditions, for it provides a valid answer to the contemporary problems of housing large numbers of spectators for athletic and cultural events without violating the University genre. Contemporary structure used also as a design element and contemporary acoustics in the form of a portable, plastic shell, set up for musical and theatrical events, have combined with the University's traditional liking of the domical form and red brick to produce a thoroughly interesting building. It has also given, because of its bulk (it will seat 9,000), a new focus to a rather nondescript landscape, a perhaps unexpected but most popular dividend. The architects were Baskervill and Son, with Anderson, Beckwith and Haible as consultants.

E26 **University of Virginia** *1817-26 Charlottesville Inquire at Rotunda*

We know from letters that Jefferson had conceived of a college as what he called an "academical village" many years before he began building the University of Virginia in 1817. Armed with suggestions from Dr. Thornton, the winner of the competition for the Capitol in Washington, and Benjamin H. Latrobe, the then Architect of the Capitol, Jefferson adapted his earlier ideas to the site and the purse of the new institution. In 1819 the Legislature designated Central College, as the school was then known, as the University of Virginia, and accepted Jefferson's plan for it. This legal acceptance of the plan was Jefferson's defense against those members of his board who later wished to change it.

The original scheme consisted of the Rotunda, housing the large classrooms and the library, at the head of an open-ended rectangle, the two sides of which contained students' rooms between the Pavilions, each of which had a classroom on the first floor and quarters for a professor on the second. The ranges of buildings on either side of this central composition housed students and the "hotels" at which the students were "dieted." The colonnades of the central group and the arcades of the flanking ranges served as sheltered connections from point to point.

All of the buildings have been extensively remodeled over the years, many of the roof forms have been changed, and only Pavilion III retains its original size. Although students and faculty still occupy the buildings, no classes are held in them at the present time. The walls of the gardens have been put back in their original position and handsome, though conjectural, plantings have been established within them by The Garden Club of Virginia.

Jefferson's scheme and its execution resulted in a unique grouping of neo-classic buildings for collegiate purposes. It has functioned so well and has been so universally admired as one of the few undoubted architectural masterpieces in this country, that it is surprising that other colleges have not built similar schemes.

E27

E28

E29

Burned in 1895, the Rotunda was put into its present condition by Stanford White. Of the original Rotunda only portions of the outer walls are left.

E27 **Stono** *1818   Lexington (432 Institute Hill) Private*

Col. John Jordan, the architect and builder of Stono, also designed the central building at Washington and Lee and the hospital at Virginia Military Institute. The central two-story mass of Stono, with its low wings, is derived from earlier practices, but its neo-classic portico marks it as a house of its own time. Here, just as at Washington and Lee, Jordan seems to have been at the mercy of his workmen, who appear incapable of having executed "correct" detail. As a result the house is full of interesting provincialisms.

E28 **Virginia Military Institute** *1848-60; 1870-73; 1914   Lexington Inquire at office*

Virginia Military Institute was designed in 1848 by Alexander Jackson Davis of New York, one of the ablest and most eminent architects in the country at that time. There was almost continual building at the Institute until 1860: the barracks from 1848-50; two villas in 1851; the mess hall in 1852; the chapel in 1859; and the Superintendent's house in 1860, all under the direction of Davis.

Burned in 1864, the Institute was rebuilt between 1870-73, again under the direction of Davis. Rebuilt once more in 1914 by Bertram Grosvenor Goodhue, it has lost some of its original romanticism. Nevertheless, Lexington is more than fortunate in having two such distinguished architectural groups as Washington and Lee and Virginia Military Institute.

The Institute, as the first castellated academic building in the country, set the tone not only for other military schools but also for armories all over the land, an influence lasting almost until the outbreak of World War II.

E29 **Washington and Lee University** *1823-42; 1930's   Lexington Inquire at office*

Although John Jordan designed the original, central building of the Washington and Lee complex, there is very little of his work left; the roof was raised and the pediment changed at a later date, and the entire interior was rebuilt during the 1930's. A plain second building was put up on one side between 1823 and 1842, then a balancing building on the other. Both were given importance by the addition of the present flat porticoes and tied to the central building by the pilastered connecting units.

In spite of the element of chance in these building operations, directed chiefly by members of the board of the university, the entire composition rests perfectly on the edge of the hill. The crispness of its white columns, piers and entablatures against the red brick save it, in spite of the provincialisms which have crept into its execution, from sentimentality. Its details are Roman, and it should be classed with earlier neo-classic buildings of the state, rather than, as some authors have assumed,

E30

E31

E32

with the then current Greek Revival.

One should also note the wooden statue of George Washington crowning the central building. It was carved by a local cabinetmaker, Matthew Kahle, and a Col. Williamson of Virginia Military Institute.

E30 **Waverly Hill** *1929   Staunton (Meadowbrook Rd.) Private*

William Lawrence Bottomley designed this beautiful, neo-Georgian house for Mr. and Mrs. Herbert McK. Smith in 1929. He poured his great knowledge of detail, proportion and invention into it. Yet the freshness of his approach and the surprise of some of his design, as in the exposed brick columns with their cast clay capitals of the loggia, keep the building from any stigma of the copyist. The landscaping was firmly controlled as well, and still plays a very strong part in the original scheme.

E31 **Western State Hospital** *1826-28   Staunton (Greenville Ave., intersection of Routes 11 and 250) Private*

The Baltimore architect William Small was brought in by the Commonwealth to design this building, still operated by the Department of Mental Hygiene and Hospitals. In this, it was simply continuing a tradition established during the previous century when Eastern State Hospital, also for mental diseases and one of the first in the country, was established at Williamsburg. The State, as client, chose the then new movement in architecture, the Greek Revival, for this triple-porticoed hospital, expressive of solidity and reliability, qualities that might have a therapeutic as well as aesthetic effect.

E32 **Woodrow Wilson Birthplace** *1846   Staunton (24 N. Coalter St.; north from junction of Routes 11 and 250) Daily, 9-5   Fee*

This charming late Greek Revival house was built as a manse for the Presbyterian church by the master builder John Fifer. As with so many houses in this hilly part of Virginia, the slope in its site allows the house an extra story on one side. In this case the modesty of the street front is replaced by the expansiveness of the garden front, with its two-story porch and garden-level kitchen and dining room. The house was carefully restored by the Woodrow Wilson Birthplace Foundation, Inc., just before World War II.

1 Peaks of Otter Lodge
2 Poplar Forest
3 Fincastle
4 Shady Grove
5 Charlotte Courthouse
6 Staunton Hill
7 Berry Hill
8 Prestwould
9 Briery Church
10 Hollins College
   Quadrangle
11 Abingdon Bank
12 Currie House
13 Smithfield Plantation
14 Public Library
15 Schoolfield-Compson
   House
16 Allied Arts Building
17 Lynchburg Courthouse
18 Hotel Roanoke
19 Patrick Henry High School

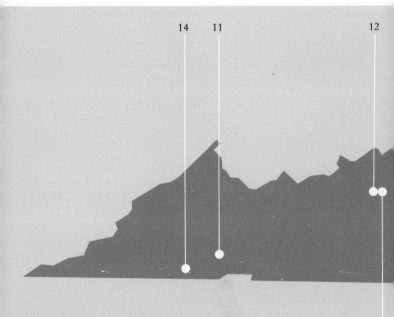

Section F Southern Virginia Introduction

Large as Virginia is today, it was almost unimaginably vast in former times, stretching over nearly half a continent. The present southwestern portion of the Commonwealth also presented a difficult terrain to both travelers and settlers, and thus was more slowly populated than its easterly portions, serving almost more as a route for pioneers than as a site for establishing oneself on the land. It is not surprising, then, that even today it is a thinly populated area. What is surprising is that its centers of commerce are vigorously thrusting to the forefront in trade, in the establishment of educational institutions and in contemporary forms of architecture. It will not be long before a body of new architecture will be established here through the demands of an enlightened clientele and the increasing prosperity of the area.

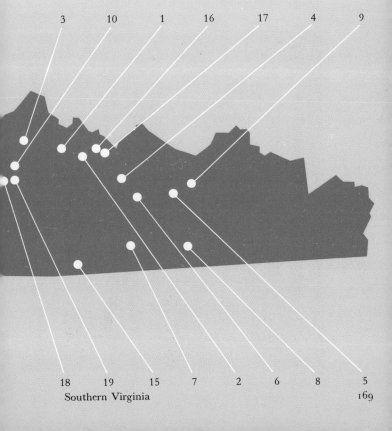

F1

F2

F3

F4

F₁   **Peaks of Otter Lodge** *1964   Bedford Co. (Junction of Route 43 & Blue Ridge Parkway) May-October*

The National Parks have had a long history of "log-cabin" lodges for the accommodation of their visitors. Now a contemporary lodge has been allowed, and Johnson, Craven and Gibson, the architects, have been most sympathetic to the National Park Service tradition of timber while using contemporary forms. Great care has been taken with every detail of this lodge, both from the point of view of color and of form. The successful result stands by a newly-made lake, which replaces an earlier marsh where evidence of Indians of some 8000 years ago was found. The lodge is operated by the Virginia Peaks of Otter Co.

F₂   **Poplar Forest** *1806; 1845; 1950's   Bedford Co. (From Lynchburg, 8 miles west on Route 460, 1 mile on Route 661, turn left ¾ mile on private road) Private*

Thomas Jefferson designed this octagonal house for himself as a summer home and a retreat from the bustle of Monticello. In it he indulged his fancy, both in his love for octagonal forms and in his use of interior ornament, a fancy, as he once said, that could not be expressed in public buildings. The octagonal forms led to some difficult interior spaces, while the interior ornament has disappeared.

On November 6, 1845, a fire began in the shingle roof, burning not only the roof but the trim of the interiors as well. The present roof with its dormers was put on immediately after the fire, but the walls, chimneys and columns are original. Mr. and Mrs. James Watts, Jr., today's owners, have made the house livable while retaining its original character.

F₃   **Fincastle** *Botetourt Co. (Route 220, 14 miles north of Roanoke)*

Fincastle is a delightful village that can still give a very good idea of the idyllic life of a small agricultural community of the first half of the 19th century. Fifty years after it was founded in 1772 there were only 63 taxable buildings. By 1835 there were 260 homes. Roman, Greek and Gothic forms appear, as well as a very late and very provincial adaptation of the Georgian. Especially noteworthy are the courthouse of 1845-48; St. Mark's (Episcopal) Church, 1837; the Methodist Church, 1840; and the Presbyterian Church, remodeled as a Greek Revival building in 1849. The most elaborate domestic woodwork is to be be found in the Kyle house of 1830-32.

Fincastle reached a peak of population in 1860 with 876 inhabitants. From that point on her population declined until it is now only 403. Though this decline is bad economically it has saved Fincastle architecturally.

F₄   **Shady Grove** *c. 1790-1814   Campbell Co. (Route 501 south from Lynchburg 18 miles to Gladys, left on Route 652 for 2 miles, left on Route 650) Private*

Though we know this house was built for Spotswood Henry and his wife Paulina Cabell, we do not know whether Patrick

F5

F6

F7

Henry built it for his son c.1790 or Dr. Cabell built it for his daughter c.1814. It has stylistic characteristics of both dates, the massing of the building belonging to the 18th century, while the detail of the dormers, the mantels and the paneling of the hall have the delicacy of the early 19th century. This wedding of styles gives the house great interest, while its rural setting preserves what must have been the original look of the site. It is now owned by Mr. and Mrs. Ennis H. Doston and Mr. and Mrs. Hugh Hight Dotson.

F5   **Courthouse** *1823   Charlotte Co. Office hours*

Unmistakably Virginian, this little temple-form courthouse, the third on the site, has the wide intercolumniation of the Jeffersonian neo-classicism. Although its exterior is not much changed, the interior has had many renovations, and is not, presumably, very close to the original. The Roman detail of the portico and entablature is rather more correct than is sometimes found in the Virginia buildings of the 1820's. Because of the appearance of the portico, the Courthouse has sometimes been attributed to Thomas Jefferson.

F6   **Staunton Hill** *1848-50   Charlotte Co. (near Brookneal) Private*

The work on Staunton Hill was carried on while its owner Charles Bruce was making the Grand Tour of Europe. His architect, John E. Johnson, because of the remote site of the house, brought in workmen from Philadelphia to execute the beautiful detail of this romantic Gothic Revival building. Mirrors were imported from Venice, and the grey marble for the portico was sent from Italy. One authority points out that Staunton Hill, with its bay windows, its stained glass, its crenellations, its clustered colonettes and its pointed arches is among the "finest Gothic Revival mansions in America," and that it has the "freedom of plan and the asymmetry that were to become the principal characteristics of modern architecture." The house is now owned by Ambassador David K. E. Bruce.

F7   **Berry Hill** *1835-40   Halifax Co. (From South Boston, 7/10 mile on 152 to 682, right 3 miles to 659, left 4 miles to house) Private*

Berry Hill was almost the last of the great houses to be built in Virginia. It was erected for James Coles Bruce in Halifax County by an unknown designer, though Mr. Bruce may have had the help of John E. Johnson. In style it is the purest of the surviving Greek Revival mansions in the State.

Its isolated site lends an almost overpoweringly romantic aura to the distinction of its carefully executed portico flanked by two small Doric pavilions. The entire composition is on as grand a scale as any of Virginia's domestic architecture, with the possible exception of the Governor's Palace at Williamsburg. It is a notable achievement, particularly when one realizes that it was carried to completion in a remote area of the Commonwealth. This isolation gives the entire composition an almost theatrical air of romanticism in spite of the classic forms of the three buildings that frame the forecourt.

F8

F9

F10

F11

174   Architecture in Virginia

F8   **Prestwould** *1794-95 Mecklenburg Co. (From Clarksville, 3 miles north on Route 15, left at marker) June, July, August, Wed and Sun., 2-5 Fee*

Invoices and bills, especially one from Jacob Shelton, the mason, for the work he had done during the 1794 season, definitely date Prestwould, although it is given a much earlier date by some authorities. Built for Sir Peyton Skipwith, the house has an unusual range of windows, a great square entrance hall with staircase with two rooms on either side and a room behind. A letter of 1795 written by Lady Skipwith ordered the hardware and inquired about wallpaper, which was installed c. 1801. The paint ordered was Spanish Brown, Stone colored, Lead colored, and White Lead. In 1800 the house was described by Wade Hampton as not having "as much gingerbread work on it as the Presidents in the city of Washington, but the materials, design, and exceutions make it altogether but little inferior to it . . . Upon the whole except about New York or up the North River I have never seen anything so handsome." The building is now owned by the Roanoke River Branch, APVA, and houses the Roanoke River Museum, the Roanoke River Chapter of the Archeaological Society of Virginia and the Roanoke River Art Association, a Chapter in the Virginia Museum's Statewide Confederation of Chapters and Affiliates.

F9   **Briery Church** *1856   Prince Edward Co. (From Farmville, Route 15 south to county line)*

Briery is the third Presbyterian church on this site. It was designed by Robert L. Dabney, its supply minister from 1856 to 1858, and he preached its dedication sermon on November 9, 1856. Its Gothic Revival aspect is in marked contrast to his classical structures at Tinkling Springs, Farmville and Hampden-Sydney. It is said the multiple doors were introduced so that one would always enter in full view of the congregation, discouraging, it was hoped, loiterers in the churchyard. This charming and rather exaggerated structure is an excellent example of mid-19th century romanticism allied with the solemnities of religion.

F10   **Hollins College Quadrangle** *1846-56   Roanoke Co. (From center of Roanoke, east on Routes 11 and 117 for 7 miles)*

The mid-19th century buildings at Hollins College amply demonstrate the charm of a simple classicism slightly tinged with early Victorianism. They are an excellent lesson in the effect to be gained from a firm sense of order combined with a judicious use of repeated but unelaborate detail. This lesson is more than valid today, especially in collegiate building, which must serve large numbers of students at reasonable cost.

F11   **Abingdon Bank** *c. 1845   Abingdon (225 E. Main St.) Private*

Used first as a bank and dwelling, this building, with its puzzling detail, partly so neo-classic and partly so Victorian, has

F12

F13

F14

F15

176   Architecture in Virginia

now been transformed entirely into a dwelling owned by Mr. W. A. Stuart. At any rate, its crispness makes it a model of 19th century urban architecture, which so frequently and so wisely combined business and domestic facilities under the same roof.

F12 **Currie House** *1961   Blacksburg (106 Highland Ave.) Private*

Built by Leonard J. Currie and designed by himself as a member of the firm of Atkins, Currie and Payne, this house takes every possible advantage of its steeply sloping site and of its structural system of support from its central core. The gently sloping, shingled roof, the exterior walls freed of the necessity of support, and the romantically geometric details give the house a distinction rarely found in today's domestic architecture. Once more imagination and intelligence demonstrate their worth. In 1963 the house received the First Honor Award in the custom-designed-house classification in the American Institute of Architects' Homes for Better Living Awards Program. The present owners are Dr. and Mrs. J. Peter Trower.

F13 **Smithfield Plantation** *1773; 1961-64   Blacksburg (¼ mile east of Route 460 on Route 314) March 15-Nov. 15, Wed., Sat., Sun., 1-5   Fee*

Smithfield, built in 1773, is, for so western a site in Virginia, an early plantation. Its outbuildings include a smoke house, summer kitchen, law office, spring house, grist mill, miller's house and barn, an incomparable array of the adjuncts necessary to a plantation house of the time and site. The house itself is a simple L-shaped, timber dwelling without much architectural pretension, just as one would expect at so remote a location. Now owned by the Association for the Preservation of Virginia Antiquities, it was recently restored by Moundfield and Guerrant, with Frederick D. Nichols as consultant.

F14 **Public Library** *1965   Bristol (James St.) Library hours, except Wed. and Sun.*

This excellent library, designed by Kearfoot and Jones, has an interesting interplay between its glass walls and those that are semi-opaque. Its strong horizontal lines are strengthened by the level grass terrace, supported by a retaining wall at the sidewalk, acting as a podium for the building in its urban setting. Fieldstone for emphasis and handsome contemporary furnishings complete this successful structure.

F15 **Schoolfield-Compson House** *1883   Danville (944 Main St.) Private*

It is said that when this house was built for John H. Schoolfield there were enough rooms in it for every member of the family to have a separate sitting room. Whether this is true or not, its careful detailing, its elongated windows, its heavy, bracketed entablature, its delicate ironwork, its Italian marble mantels, its plaster rosettes and moldings imported from France and its brass and crystal chandeliers all contribute to its positive expression of the Victorian sense of style. Now owned by Mr. and

F16

F17

F18

F19

Mrs. R. Michael Compson, it has had a rear porch filled in, a new rear porch added, and a portion of the house has been turned into an apartment.

F16 **Allied Arts Building** *1930-31   Lynchburg (725 Church St.)*

The early modernism of the Allied Arts Building, built of steel, buff brick and greenstone taken from a quarry within the city limits of Lynchburg, was a considerable achievement for the depression years, and its clean lines and sharp silhouette give it great character today. The architects, Stanhope S. Johnson and Ray O. Brannan, turned the difficulty of its hilly site and its narrow, forty-foot frontage on the major street to considerable dramatic use, while its 17 stories continue to dominate Lynchburg. It is still in the hands of the original owners, the Allied Arts Building Corporation.

F17 **Courthouse** *1855   Lynchburg (9th & Court Sts.) Office hours*

Standing on land given by John Lynch, founder of Lynchburg, the present courthouse is the second to occupy the site. It is also the focal point of a great stair of 139 steps leading up to its street level. Though its walls are masonry covered with stucco, its Greek Revival columns and entablature are worked out in wood. Its designer, either Andrew Ellison, Jr., or perhaps W. S. Ellison, made good use of the heavy Greek proportions in gaining dominance for his building on its imposing site. It was completed May 25, 1855, by Hallet and Mace for $22,000.

F18 **Hotel Roanoke** *1882; 1931; 1937; 1947; 1955   Roanoke*

Built and owned by the Norfolk and Western Railway, the Hotel Roanoke began as a Victorian, half-timbered building, housing both offices and some of the Norfolk and Western workmen. After a fire in 1916, the present building was erected in stages, the half-timbering of the earlier building being retained in the new structure. There are now 425 rooms in the hotel, which has maintained a splendid style and a high standard of comfort over many decades and through many rebuildings and additions.

F19 **Patrick Henry High School** *1963   Roanoke (Grandin Rd.) School hours*

Designed by Caudill, Rowlett and Scott in association with Smithey and Boynton, Patrick Henry High School is an example of the campus type of school. Classes are housed in three buildings holding 400 students each, while the gym, cafeteria, and library are housed in the other two buildings. The excellent planning and the forthright use of structural elements have given Roanoke a school both impressive and contemporary, two qualities not necessarily synonymous.

Bibliographies
by Frederick D. Nichols

General

Architects' Emergency Committee. *Great Georgian Houses of America*. New York: 1933.

Bannister, T. C., ed. *The Architect at Mid-Century, Evolution and Achievement*. New York: 1954.

Beirne, R. R. and J. H. Scharff. *William Buckland, 1731-1774, Architect of Virginia and Maryland*. Baltimore: 1958.

Bridenbaugh, Carl. *The Colonial Craftsman*. New York: 1950.

Burchard, John and Albert Bush-Brown. *The Architecture of America*. Boston: 1961.

Claiborne, H. A. *Comments on Virginia Brickwork before 1800*. Boston: 1957.

Dearstyne, H. B. "Shutters, Blinds and Umbrelloes," *Architectural Review*, CXXIII (June, 1958), 402-22.

Donnell, Edna. "A. J. Davis and the Gothic Revival," *Metropolitan Museum Studies*, V (1936), 183-233.

Dowdey, C. *The Great Plantation: A Profile of Berkeley Hundred and Plantation Virginia from Jamestown to Appomattox*. N. Y.: 1957.

Farr, Finis, "The Countenance of Principle," *Arts in Virginia*, III (Fall, 1962), 2-9.

Frary, I. T. *Thomas Jefferson, Archt. and Builder*. Richmond: 1931.

Gutheim, Frederick. "Dead Centers," *Arts in Virginia*, III (Spring, 1963). 14-21.

Hamlin, Talbot. *Benjamin Henry Latrobe*. New York: 1955.

_____. *Greek Revival Architecture in America*. New York: 1944.

Howells, J. M. *Lost Examples of Colonial Architecture*. N. Y.: 1931.

Kimball, Fiske. "Form and Function in the Architecture of Jefferson," *Magazine of Art*, XL (April, 1947), 150-53.

_____. *Thomas Jefferson, Architect: Original Designs in the Collection of Thomas Jefferson Coolidge, Jr.* Cambridge, Mass.: 1916.

Kocher, A. L., and H. B. Dearstyne. *Shadows in Silver: A Record of Virginia, 1850-1900*. New York: 1954.

Major, Howard. *The Domestic Architecture of the Early American Republic: The Greek Revival*. Philadelphia and London: 1926.

Milhollen, H. D. *Old Virginia Court Houses*. Alexandria, Va.: 1942.

Nichols, F. D. "The Early Architecture of Virginia: Original Sources and Books," *in* W. B. O'Neal, ed. *The American Association of Architectural Bibliographers: Papers, Vol. I.* Charlottesville, Va.: 1965; "The Early Architecture of Virginia: Journals," *ibid.*, Vol. II. Charlottesville, Va.: 1966.

_____. *Thomas Jefferson's Architectural Drawings*. Boston: 1959. 2nd. ed., Boston and Charlottesville: 1961.

_____. and W. B. O'Neal. *Architecture in Virginia, 1776-1958: The Old Dominion's Twelve Best Buildings:* Richmond: 1958.

_____. "The Restoration of Colonial Architecture in Virginia," *U. of Virginia News Letter*, XXXVII (March 15, 1961), 25-27.

O'Neal, William B. "Town and Country, Garden and Field," *Arts in Virginia*, IV (Fall, 1963), 18-25.

Pratt, Dorothy and Richard Pratt, *A Guide to Early American Homes, South*. New York: 1956.

Pratt, Richard. *Second Treasury of Early American Homes*. N.Y.: 1954.

————. *A Treasury of Early American Homes*. New York: 1949.

Rawlings, James Scott. *Virginia's Colonial Churches: An Architectural Guide*. Richmond: 1963.

Rose, H. W. *Churches of Colonial America*. New York: 1963.

Shurtleff, H. R. *The Log Cabin Myth*. Cambridge, Mass.: 1939.

Waterman, T. T. "Architecture of the American Indians," *American Anthropologist*, XXIX (April-June, 1927), 210-30.

Section A   The Richmond Area

Howland, R. H. "Echoes of a Gilded Epoch," *Arts in Virginia*, V (Fall, 1964), 2-9.

Kimball, Fiske. "Jefferson and the Public Buildings of Virginia: II—Richmond, 1779-1780," *Huntington Library Quarterly*, XII (May, 1949), 303-10.

"The Ladies Move a Mansion: The Colonial Dames Rescued Wilton from Destruction," *Virginia Cavalcade*, XV (Spring, 1966), 9-17.

McCormick, Thomas J. "Virginia's Gallic Godfather," *Arts in Virginia*, IV (Winter, 1964), 2-13.

Meeks, C. L. V. "Character, Ugliness, Beauty and Time," *Arts in Virginia*, II (Spring, 1962), 12-21.

O'Neal, William B. "The Multiple Life of Space," *Arts in Virginia*, V (Spring, 1965), 2-11.

Rice, A. Bransford. "A Portfolio of Wilton," *Virginia Cavalcade*, XVC (Spring, 1966), 18-29.

Scott, M. W. "Cast Iron Ornament in Richmond," *Arts in Virginia*, II (Winter, 1962), 20-29.

————. *Old Richmond Neighborhoods*. Richmond: 1950.

————. and L. F. Catterall. *Virginia's Capitol Square: Its Buildings and Its Monuments*. Richmond: 1957.

Seymour, Charles, Jr. "Early Republican Masterpiece," *Arts in Virginia*, II (Winter, 1962), 4-17.

Section B   The James River Area

Bailey, J. H. "The Greek Revival in Petersburg," *Virginia Cavalcade*, VII (Winter, 1957), 33-39.

Byrd, William. *Another Secret Diary of William Byrd of Westover, 1739-1741*. Ed. by M. H. Woodfin and Marion Tinling. Richmond, Va.: 1942.

————. *The Secret Diary of William Byrd of Westover, 1709-1712*. Ed. by L. B. Wright and Marion Tinling. Richmond: 1941.

Butt, M. W. *Portsmouth under Four Flags*, 1752-1961. Portsmouth, Va.: 1961.

Goodwin, T. R. *A Brief and True Report Concerning Williamsburg in Virginia*. Williamsburg, Va.: 1941.

"Governor's Palace, Colonial Williamsburg," *Architectural Record*, LXXVIII (Dec., 1935), 378-81; LXXX (Nov., 1935), 354-63, 370-71.

Hulton, P. H. *The American Drawings of John White*. Chapel Hill, N. C.: 1964.

Kellan, S. S. *Old Houses in Princess Anne*. Portsmouth, Va.: 1931.

Kimball, Fiske. "Jefferson and the Public Buildings of Virginia: I—Williamsburg, 1707-1776," *Huntington Library Quarterly*, XII (Feb., 1949), 115-20.

_____. "Restoration of Colonial Williamsburg." *Architectural Record*, LXXVIII (Dec., 1935), 359.

Kocher, A. L., and H. B. Dearstyne. *Colonial Williamsburg: Its Buildings and Gardens*. Williamsburg, Va.: 1945.

Mason, G. C. *Colonial Churches of Tidewater Virginia*. Richmond, Va.: 1945.

Meeks, C. L. V. "Lynx and Phoenix: Litchfield and Williamsburg," *Journal of the Society of Architectural Historians*, X (No. 4, 1951), 18-23.

Moorehead, S. P. "Tazewell Hall: A Report on Its 18th Century Appearance," *Journal of the Society of Architectural Historians*, XIV (March, 1955), 14-17.

Riley, E. M., and C. E. Hatch, Jr. *James Towne in the Words of Contemporaries*. Washington: 1955 (i.e., 1956).

Troubetskoy, U. "Welcome to Shirley," *Virginia Cavalcade*, IX (Autumn, 1959), 9-17.

Van Derpool, J. G. "The Restoration of St. Luke's, Smithfield, Virginia," *Journal of the Society of Architectural Historians*, XVII (No. 1, 1958), 12-18.

Whiffen, Marcus. *The Eighteenth Century Houses of Williamsburg: A Study of Architecture and Buildings in the Colonial Capital of Virginia*. New York: 1960.

_____. *The Public Buildings of Williamsburg*. Williamsburg, Va.: 1958.

Section C   The Rappahannock Area

Embrey, A. T. *History of Fredericksburg*. Richmond, Va.: 1932. *Kenmore, 1752*. Fredericksburg, Va.: 1965.

Nichols, Frederick D. "Stratford Hall," *Arts in Virginia*, VII (Spring, 1967), 24-31.

Waterman, Thomas Tilestone. "Rosewell, Gloucester County," *Architectural Forum*, LII (Jan., 1930), 17-20.

Section D   Northern Virginia

Alexandria Assoc. *Our Town, 1749-1865*. Alexandria, Va.: 1956.

Halsey, R. T. H., R. T. Haines and C. O. Cornelius. *Handbook of the American Wing*. N. Y.: 1925. 2nd ed., 1938.

Kimball, Fiske. "Gunston Hall," *Journal of the Society of Architectural Historians*, XIII (May, 1954), 3-8.

Lindsey, Mary. *Historic Homes and Landmarks of Alexandria, Va.* Alexandria, Va.: 1931.

Moore, G. M. *Seaport in Virginia: Washington's Alexandria*. Richmond, Va.: 1949.

Nelligan, Murray. "The Building of Arlington House," *Journal of the Soc. of Arch. Historians*, X (No. 2, 1951), 11-15.

Thane, Elswyth. *Mount Vernon Is Ours*. New York: 1966.

"Virginia Architecture in the Jet Age," *Arts in Virginia*, I (Winter, 1961), 2-9.

Von Eckardt, Wolf. "Planning for 'Publick Concerns'," *Arts in Virginia*, VII (Winter, 1967), 16-29.

Section E   The Piedmont Area

Bosserman, J. Norwood. "A Shrine Preserved," *Arts in Virginia*, V (Winter, 1965), 6-11.

Couper, Col. William. *One Hundred Years at Virginia Military Institute*. Richmond, Va.: 1940.

Cox, Warren. "The Mood of a Great Campus: Jefferson's Buildings at the University of Virginia," *Architectural Forum*, Feb., 1962, pp. 74 ff.

Dickenson, J. L. *The Fairfax Proprietary: The Northern Neck, the Fairfax Manors, and the Beginnings of Warren County in Virginia*. Front Royal, Va.: 1959.

"Goochland Courthouse," *Virginia Magazine of History and Biography*, XLIV (July, 1936), 243.

Kimball, Fiske. "The Building of Bremo," *Virginia Magazine of History and Biography*, LVII (Jan., 1949), 3-13.

Meade, Everard W. "Sophistication in the Wilderness," *Arts in Virginia*, II (Fall, 1961), 22-29.

Nichols, Frederick D. "Phoenix in Virginia," *Arts in Virginia*, I (Spring, 1961), 22-29.

_____. "Viewmont," *Magazine of Albemarle County History*, XIII (1953), 23-27.

_____. "The Restoration of 'Academical Village' Gardens Completed," *University of Virginia Alumni News*, LIII (March-April, 1965), 2-7, 31-33.

O'Neal, William B. "A Checklist of Writings on Thomas Jefferson as an Architect," *American Association of Architectural Bibliographers*, Fall, 1959.

_____. *Jefferson's Buildings at the University of Virginia: The Rotunda*. Charlottesville, Va.: 1960.

_____. *Jefferson's Fine Arts Library for the University of Virginia*. Charlottesville, Va.: 1956.

_____. "Origins of the University Ground Plans," *University of Virginia Alumni News*, L (Nov., 1962), 4-7.

Percy, Alfred. *The Amherst County Story: A Virginia Saga*. Madison Heights, Va.: 1961.

Rawlings, Mary. *Albemarle of Other Days*. Charlottesville, Va.: 1925.

_____. *Ante-bellum Albemarle*. Charlottesville, Va.: 1935.

Reniers, Percival. *The Springs of Virginia*. Chapel Hill, N.C.: 1941.

_____. "Taking the Waters in Style," *Arts in Virginia*, III (Winter, 1963), 12-17.

Troubetzkoy, U. "Tuckahoe Plantation," *Virginia Cavalcade*, X (Spring, 1961), 5-12.

Section F   Southern Virginia

Hairston, L. B. W. *A Brief History of Danville*. Rich., Va.: 1955.

Nichols, Frederick D. "Mansions That Merchandising Built," *Arts in Virginia*, VI (Spring, 1966), 12-21.

Niederer, Frances J. "Fincastle's Revival Architecture," *ibid.*, VI (Winter, 1966), 12-19.

Richardson, E. R., ed. *Roanoke: Story of County and City*. Roanoke, Va.: 1942.

Turner, S. M. "The Skipwiths of Prestwould Plantation," *Virginia Cavalcade*, X (Summer, 1960), 42-47.

Chronological Index
Note: Only the first dates of buildings are given.

1818, Carrington Row, Richmond, 27
1818, Stono, Lexington, 165
1819-34, Fort Monroe, Old Point Comfort, 63-65
1820, Bremo, Fluvanna Co., 155
1820, National Bank of Fredericksburg, Fredericksburg, 117
1820, Upper Brandon, Prince George Co., 59
1821, Oak Hill, Loudoun Co., 131
1823, Courthouse, Charlotte Co., 173
1823-42, Washington and Lee University, Lexington, 165-67
1824, Bell Tower, Richmond, 25
c. 1825, Hampstead, New Kent Co., 55-57
c. 1825, Powhatan, King George Co., 105-7
1826, Courthouse, Goochland Co., 155
1826-28, Western State Hospital, Staunton, 167
1827-32, Old Norfolk Naval Hospital, Portsmouth, 75
1828, Courthouse, Madison Co., 157
c. 1830, Downtown Baptist Church, Alexandria, 135
1830-32, Kyle House, Fincastle, 171
1830-35, Morris Cottages, Richmond, 27
c. 1832, Mirador, Albemarle Co., 149
1835, Old Humpback Bridge, Allegheny Co., 151-158
1835, Warehouse Building, Navy Yard, Portsmouth, 77
1835-40, Berry Hill, Halifax Co., 173
1836, Women's Bath House, Warm Springs, Bath Co., 153
1837, St. Mark's Church, Fincastle, 171
1838, Courthouse, Greene Co., 157
1839-40, Exchange Building, Petersburg, 73
1840, Methodist Church, Fincastle, 171
1840, Old Norfolk Academy, Norfolk, 71
1840, Vowell-Smith House, Alexandria, 141
1841, Glasgow House, Richmond, 31
1841, Old First Baptist Church, Richmond, 41
1844, Tabb Street Presbyterian Church, Petersburg, 75
1844-45, St. Paul's Episcopal Church, Richmond, 43
1845, Egyptian Building, Richmond, 19, 29
c. 1845, Abingdon Bank, Abingdon, 175-77
1845-48, Courthouse, Botetourt Co., 171
1846, Woodrow Wilson Birthplace, Staunton, 167
1846-56, Hollins College Quadrangle, 175
1847, Hollywood Cemetery, Richmond, 33
1847, Linden Row, Richmond, 13, 37
1847-50, General Douglas MacArthur Memorial, Norfolk, 69
1848-50, Staunton Hill, Charlotte Co., 173
1848-60, Virginia Military Institute, Lexington, 165
1849, Hardgrove House, Richmond, 27
1849, Presbyterian Church, Fincastle, 171
1849-50, Freemason Street Baptist Church, Norfolk, 67-69
1850, Baptist Church, Waterford, 131
c. 1850, Ironwork, Richmond, 33
1851-52, Courthouse, Fredericksburg, 115
1852, Customs House, Norfolk, 13, 67
c. 1852-58, Courthouse, Orange Co., 159
1853, Grant Tobacco Factory, Richmond, 31
1853, Morson's Row, Richmond, 41
1855, Courthouse, Lynchburg, 179
1855-59, United States Post Office, Richmond, 45
1856, Briery Church, Prince Edward Co., 175
1857-59, Camden, Caroline Co., 97
1858, Armistead House, Williamsburg, 83
1858, Bolling-Haxall House, Richmond, 21
1859, Mayhurst, Orange Co., 159
1860, Broad Street Methodist Church, Richmond, 23
c. 1865, Iron Fronts, Richmond, 33
1866, Branch and Co., Richmond, 21

General Index

Note: This index lists only the names of towns, buildings, architects, contractors, craftsmen and suppliers. The names of architectural firms are listed only in their usual form.

Photographic Credits

Cover: William Francis.

Introduction: 1, Colonial Williamsburg, courtesy Virginia State Library; 2, Thomas L. Williams, courtesy Jamestown Foundation; 3, 4, 5, 6, 7, 10, Ronald Jennings, courtesy University of Virginia; 9, Norfolk Museum; 8, 11, 12, 13, 14, Virginia State Library; 15, The Valentine; 16, 17, 19, Gordon Burris; 18, Ronald Jennings, courtesy Marcellus Wright & Partners.

Section A: Intro, 10, 21, Virginia State Library; 1, 3, 4, 5, 6, 8b 11, 13, 17, 20, 22, 23, 25, 29, 31, 36, 39, 40, 41, 42, 44, Ronald Jennings; 2, 15, 16, 18, 45b, Dementi Studio; 7, 9, 14, 19, 26, 27, 32, 33, 34, 35, 45a, 46, Richard Cheek; 8a, 12, Virginia Chamber of Commerce; 24, William Francis; 28, 30, Gordon Burris; 37, Reynolds Metals Company; 38, 43, Colonial Studio.

Section B: Intro, Mariners Museum, courtesy Jamestown Foundation; 1, 2, 3, 4, 5, 6a, 7a, 7b, 9, 10, 12, 13, 15, 41, 42, Virginia Chamber of Commerce; 6b, Williamsburg Intro, 43-59, Colonial Williamsburg; 8, 14, 18, 19, 23, 24, 25, 26, 27, 28, 29, 31, 32, 33, 34, 36, 37, 38, 39, 40, Richard Cheek; 11, Virginia State Library; 16, 17, National Park Service; 20, Ronald Jennings; 21, Vincent G. Kling & Associates; 22, Gordon Burris; 30, Virginia National Bank; 35, Petersburg Chamber of Commerce.

Section C: Intro, 2, 10, 16, 19, Virginia State Library; 3, 4, 5, 7, 8, 11, 12, 13, 14, 15, 17, 18, 20, 21, 22, 24, 25, 26, 29, 30, 31, 33, 1, Richard Cheek; 6, 9, 23, 28, Virginia Chamber of Commerce; 27, Ronald Jennings; 32, A. Wilson Embree, III.

Section D: Intro, 6, 11, 20, Virginia State Library; 1, 5, 7, 12, 29, Virginia Chamber of Commerce; 2, Dementi Studio; 3, 10, 14, 17, 19, 28, 30, 31, 32, 33, 34, Richard Cheek; 4, Modernage, courtesy National Park Service; 8, National Trust; 9, Loudoun County Department of Economic and Industrial Development; 13, William J. McDonald, courtesy Waterford Foundation; 15, 16, 18, 23, 24, 25, 26, 27, J. Alexander Studio, courtesy Alexandria Chamber of Commerce; 21, 22, Charles M. Goodman Associates.

Section E: Intro, Ronald Jennings, courtesy University of Virginia; 1, 2, 7, 13, 15, Virginia State Library; 3, 12, 22, 23, 24, 27, 30, Ronald Jennings; 4, 11, 21, 32, Virginia Chamber of Commerce; 5, 6, 5, 6, 26, 28, 29, Gordon Burris; 9, 10, 16, 17, 18, 19, 20, 31, 14, 25, Richard Cheek; 10, John M. Gazzola.

Section F: Intro, 5, 8, 9, Virginia State Library; 1, Richard Cheek; 2, Virginia Chamber of Commerce; 3, William Francis; 4, 6, 10, 11, 13, 14, 15, 17, 19, Ronald Jennings; 7, Gordon Burris; 12, Leonard J. Currie; 16, Gene Campbell; 18, Norfolk & Western Railway Company.